11 March
1 April

WITHDRAWN FOR SALE

Quercus Editions Ltd
55 Baker Street
7th floor, South Block
London
W1U 8EW

First published in 2015

A catalogue record of this book is available from the British Library

ISBN 9781848669628

Printed in Great Britain by Clays Ltd, St Ives Plc

10 9 8 7 6 5 4 3 2 1

Editorial and design by Bookworx

Contents

A note from the authors

We live in ever-changing times and sometimes life can be tough. We're constantly being pulled in different directions and can struggle to cope with the pressure that we're put under by external factors and, most importantly, by ourselves. With greater choice comes greater responsibility and occasionally this can be a breeding ground for stress, unhappiness and self-doubt. There are very few people (if any at all) who feel they operate perfectly in their work, relationships and life in general. Most of us could use some help now and then – a nudge to show us how to improve our mood, to change our approach to life and to feel more content. All too often we can suffer from a sense that life is passing us by, that we're just going through the motions. Mindfulness will put a stop to lost hours, days, months or even years by ensuring you're actually present in your experiences, not just stuck in your head.

The *This Book Will* series aims to help you understand why you feel, think and behave the way you do and then gives you the tools to make positive changes. We're not fans of complicated medical jargon so we've tried to make everything accessible, relevant and entertaining as we know you'll want to see improvements as soon as possible. We draw on our professional experience and the latest research, using anecdotes and examples which we found helpful and hope you will too. Titles are split into particular subjects such as happiness, body image, mindfulness and stress, so you can focus on the areas you'd most like to address.

Built around a mindfulness-based cognitive therapy framework (MBCT), this concise, practical guide will show you how to incorporate mindfulness into your life so you become more aware of yourself and the world around you. MBCT is an incredibly successful therapy that's easy to follow, enabling you to cope with whatever life throws at you, making stressful experiences manageable and good experiences even better.

Within all of our books you'll regularly come across diagrams called mind maps. We use these to illustrate how your thoughts, behaviour, mood and body are all connected. Filling these in will break any problem down so that it doesn't seem overwhelming, while laying out options for making changes.

There are strategies and checklists throughout to guide you through the practical steps of becoming more mindful. We'll make it easy for these changes to become part of your routine because reading the theory is only going to get you so far. The only way to ensure you'll become more mindful long-term is to put everything you learn into practice and change how you experience your day-to-day life.

You can choose to feel better and live life differently and this book will show you how.

Good luck! Let us know how you get on by contacting us via our website: www.jessamyandjo.com

Jessamy and Jo

Introduction

Multitasking is a wonderful thing. In today's 24/7 society the ability to be able to send an email and talk to someone on the phone while holding a coffee as you walk down the street is a talent admired and sought after. But should it be?

We wear many different faces day-to-day: partner, parent, colleague, sibling, boss, friend, son, daughter, teacher, student – the list goes on and on. In each of these roles we try to live up to both our own expectations and those of other people. This constant pressure means days, weeks, months and even years can pass by in a blur as we try to keep up with our responsibilities. You can find yourself constantly waiting for your life – the life you're meant to be living – to start.

Life moves so quickly now – mobile phones, tablets, wifi and the propagation of 3G (and even 4G) networks mean information is immediately accessible and as a result our attention spans are getting shorter. (A recent Associated Press study found American adults now have an eight-second attention span online, down 25 per cent from 2000, while separate research found UK adults swap between technological gadgets up to 21 times an hour.) Gone are the days when you'd just watch a TV show. Now you'll read an online review before changing channel, look up the lead actor and tweet witty asides all the way through it.

This instant accessibility means there's an expectation of availability, so you rarely, if ever, 'clock off'. You can't even escape the world on holiday as you're expected to Instagram pictures of what you're eating, wearing and seeing. Go to a sporting event or gig and you'll see people recording the entire thing on their phones and watching it on the tiny screen rather than right in front of them in reality! It's no wonder people feel cut adrift if they're without technology for a day.

The frenetic pace of most of our lives can not only leave us feeling stressed, rushed and anxious, but it can also mean we forget to take a moment to simply...be. Many of us have lost the ability to actually experience the life we're living; instead we're constantly waiting, planning or worrying about the next thing on our to-do list or dwelling on the past.

When was the last time you actually savoured the taste of your lunch without worrying about that upcoming phone call/meeting/interview?

When was the last time you walked down the street observing the scenery without checking what some guy you haven't spoken to in 15 years did over the weekend on Facebook?

When was the last time you enjoyed a night out without following a list of rules you've set yourself: 'I can't mention that', 'I won't drink too much', 'I can't have a pudding', 'I have to laugh at all their jokes'?

'A wealth of information creates a poverty of attention.' Nobel Prize-winning economist Herbert Simon said this all the way back in pre-internet 1977; a statement that strikes an even louder chord now than it did then, proving why mindfulness is so relevant and important.

What is mindfulness?

Mindfulness is a practice of awareness. It's a technique for learning to become more aware of:

+ Your thoughts
+ Your emotions
+ Your body
+ Your impulses and urges
+ The world around you

It's not some airy-fairy nonsense; it's a psychological and behavioural philosophy based on hundreds of years of study in Eastern traditions that has been proven to reduce symptoms of low mood, anxiety, stress and depression. It will teach you to become more in tune with your thoughts, so you can stop them steamrolling through your head causing knee-jerk reactions. You'll start noticing the stories your mind tells you, giving you a choice about whether to listen to them or not. Mindfulness also teaches you to become more aware of your body. How you react physically to events and emotions is one of the most obvious signals of emotional distress we have, yet it's shocking how often we completely ignore or dismiss tension, aches and pains.

Most importantly, mindfulness will offer you the chance to stop living in your head. We all spend so much time planning for the future, worrying about how and what's going to happen while ruminating on the past that we forget to live in the present, to fully experience what's happening now both in and around us.

If you're open-minded to it, mindfulness will reacquaint you with yourself so you can better deal with tough times and fully enjoy good times.

Why choose this book?

This Book Will Make You Mindful is a straightforward introduction to mindfulness with anecdotes throughout helping to explain the theory. There's no waffle, no sitting around for hours in the lotus position (unless you want there to be) and no self-indulgent rambling. We've tried to make it as simple, coherent and accessible as possible so the next time you're left on hold to the electricity company for twenty minutes you'll only smash the phone to pieces against the nearest wall after taking a moment to decide you really want to.

There are two types of mindfulness: informal and formal. The term 'informal' covers the stuff you do as you go about your daily business, while 'formal' covers the meditative practices. There can be a stigma attached to meditation – that it's only for people who wear hemp coats or is in some way cultish or religious – but that's outdated and ridiculous.

Now more than ever people need a way to cope with the daily demands they're under. Mindfulness is a brilliant way of getting to know yourself better. You'll be able to de-clutter your mind and recognise how and why you think, feel and behave the way you do. That understanding will enable you to make changes, if necessary, so you can better cope with stressful events and better appreciate the here and now.

How it all works

This book is a mindfulness starter-kit rather than a course to follow. It'll teach you the philosophies behind the practice with straightforward strategies in each chapter that you can incorporate into everyday life. This is for people who are interested in gaining a better understanding of the topic, who sometimes feel that life can be overwhelming and who want to feel happier, more content, peaceful and in control. (Please be aware that we're not teaching the eight-week mindfulness-based cognitive therapy [MBCT] course. If that's what you're after there are courses listed at the back of the book.)

The book is built around the pioneering work of Dr Jon Kabat-Zinn, creator of the mindfulness-based stress-reduction programme from which Mark Williams, John Teasdale and Zindel Segal developed MBCT (all of which are discussed further in Chapter 1). We also draw on Christine Dunkley and Dr Maggie Stanton's work as well as the teachings of Vietnamese Zen Buddhist monk Thích Nhất Hạnh, a master of mindfulness.

How to get the most out of this book

+ Follow the chapters in order as each one builds on the last with the difficulty level of each strategy gradually increasing. Once you've read all the way through you can dip in and out as you need
+ Do the strategies! The strategies are all identified with an ⑤
  It's all too easy to think, 'Yeah, I'll do that later,' and skim-read

everything. This only works if you put the theory into practice. You wouldn't just read a book on how to drive and then leap into a car convinced you're a potential Formula One champion (at least we hope you wouldn't). Research shows that you learn most from doing: practising, making a few mistakes and then practising some more

+ Keep it simple: start with one strategy and practise several times a week, ideally on consecutive days to keep up momentum. When you feel you're getting the hang of it move onto the next

+ We have used and adapted strategies from a variety of sources, all of which are either cited in the text or in the references section at the back of the book

+ Some chapters will start with a strategy straight away. This is so that after you've tried it, you can use your own experience to understand and make sense of the theory behind it

+ Get a notebook and dedicate it to mindfulness. There are strategies in the book where you'll need to jot down notes and being able to flick back and see how far you've come will be really motivational. Also, writing things down aids memory and makes them more 'official' in your head

+ Remember, mindfulness isn't a quick fix; it's a skill that has to be acquired just like tennis, drawing or skiing. You won't become an expert at it immediately, so don't get angry if things don't click into place straight away. Have patience and practise

Mindfulness works best if you make a commitment both to it and to yourself as it requires time and energy, but if you stick with it the rewards are huge. You'll feel more engaged with your life, more present in everything you do. You'll be better able to deal with upsetting or stressful things and more able to enjoy the great, exciting, wonderful things. You also won't have to worry about waking up one day and suddenly wondering how ten years slid past without you noticing.

If you leave all scepticism at the door mindfulness will make your life happier. There is no way getting to know your mind better could ever be a bad thing. Give it a go – a real go – and we're convinced you'll become a convert.

1

It's All in the Mind

What is mindfulness? How can it make a real difference to your life? In this chapter we explain the philosophy behind the practice and kick things off with some starter strategies.

What is mindfulness and how can it help you?

Mindfulness is a practice of awareness, helping you to become more focused on the present, on the life you're actually living rather than a past that's been and gone and a future that hasn't arrived yet. It's about choosing what to pay attention to, rather than aimlessly following your mind's version of events. It teaches you to notice your mind's habits and ways of working, giving you a choice in whether you wish to act on its advice.

By becoming more aware of what's going on in your own head and body, you'll be able to stop your thoughts and feelings consuming you, sweeping you away on a tidal wave of stress, anxiety, fear or regret and causing you to behave in unhelpful ways. Being mindful means acknowledging your current thoughts and emotions without judgement, for example, accepting that thoughts are just thoughts, feelings are just feelings and that they don't define who you are. Mindfulness gives you choices: 'Does that really matter?' or 'Do I really want to do that?'

Learning to identify specific thoughts and moods and understanding their effects will allow you to live in the moment, to appreciate life, to choose how you want to live and to be aware of the here and now rather than steaming through and missing all the good bits.

When you're juggling a million different things, each with URGENT scribbled next to it on your to-do list, days can merge together and you

Example: Tom's tantrum

Tom only had half an hour to run down the road and buy the ingredients for the bolognese he'd promised to make his girlfriend. He arrived sweaty and dishevelled at the supermarket to find a man wearing a stupid hat picking up the last packet of mince from the shelves. He sprinted to the butcher's, only to discover that he didn't have any cash and their card machine had broken. He then dragged himself to the cashpoint, scuffing his new shoes on ....

∴ the curb on the way. And then it started to rain. 'This is just typical!' he raged. 'This always happens to me. This would never have happened to my girlfriend!' and he promptly called her and blamed her for the whole sorry saga.

If Tom was being mindful he would have recognised the anger building inside him, both in his mind and body. Simply being aware of this would have given him some much-needed distance from it. All too often we follow our mind's version of events and let our emotions devour us completely. His rampaging thoughts are actually working against him, evoking strong emotional and physical sensations that do nothing to solve the problem of the missing mince. By stepping back from his rage, Tom would have been able to then choose his reaction, so rather than getting swept up in it and calling his girlfriend, he could ask himself, 'Is that a good idea?' and wrestle back control. He then (probably) wouldn't choose to rant at her.

end up just going through the motions. Or, like Tom, you can react to stress in ways that only aggravate your anxiety and bad mood.

It's common for thoughts to be consumed by worries ('They're judging me'), plans for the future ('Everything will be great when I get a new job') or ruminations on the past ('I wish I hadn't done that'), leaving you feeling dissatisfied. You may feel as if something's missing in your life, but you can't quite put your finger on what. Mindfulness pioneer Dr Jon Kabat-Zinn summarises this edginess nicely: 'We might have a strong intuition on occasion that what is really missing in some profound way is us – our willingness or ability to show up fully in our lives and live them as if they really mattered, in the only moment we ever get'.

Mindfulness will teach you not to be numb to the world or yourself. If you really invest in mindfulness it can change your life. You'll feel more productive, more excited and more in control. The more productive bit is

> **Mindfulness in a nutshell**
>
> Mindfulness is learning to live in the present moment and taking notice of what's happening around you and in your own head, enabling you to better cope with stress and enjoy life more.

really important – because you're actually focused on what you're doing rather than tuning in to irrelevant thoughts, you'll find you get things done far more effectively and quickly. Mindfulness will actually save you time in the long run, which is worth remembering if thoughts like, 'I don't have time for this' pop into your head when considering the strategies.

Back to the future

It can be all too easy to constantly look ahead: 'One more day until Friday', 'Three more weeks until my holiday', 'Life will be better when I lose some weight'. Living constantly for the future means you never appreciate what's happening now and life passes you by. Inevitably when the weekend does arrive or when you do lose some weight you think, 'I can't believe it's Monday tomorrow' or 'Perhaps I need to lose a few more pounds'.

We all do it, but when you see it broken down like that it's actually pretty sad. You're so focused on the future that you're actually missing your life now. It's just like the famous line from the John Lennon song 'Beautiful Boy': 'Life is what happens to you while you're busy making other plans'.

Sometimes we try so hard to be happy that we end up missing the point of what true happiness is. For example, 'I'll feel great when I change jobs, join a gym, get a perfect partner, go on holiday'. If you don't achieve these goals you feel bad about yourself and sometimes, even when you do tick them off your list, you don't feel quite as great as you thought you would. Things are different, but you still feel the same. Why? Because there isn't one thing on earth that will magically make you happy, peaceful and content if you don't know what happiness, peace and contentment are to you.

If you only ever look ahead, never appreciating what you have and what you're experiencing, you'll keep moving the goalposts, making plan after plan, always waiting for your life to start. 'Things will be great after I get this promotion' or 'I'll relax after I win this award'. We're not saying you shouldn't make goals or plans – they just shouldn't come at the expense of the present. You can work towards goals while still appreciating your everyday life. Mindfulness is about living in the moment and learning how to feel contentment in what you've got now. Once you can do that, achieving those goals will feel far better than they ever could before because you're already enjoying your life.

Our minds don't only get obsessed with the future, it's also human nature to dwell on the past. To mull over things that went wrong or didn't pan out as planned. Regrets get you nowhere. You can't change the past; you can only learn from it. By ruminating on bygone days you're again missing out on real life – on all the amazing things happening right now (or the amazing things that could be happening if only you could engage with them).

Sometimes you try so hard to be happy that you actually miss happiness when it does happen: spending your birthday party worrying whether everyone else is having a good time; spending the family meal you organised thinking about the big presentation at work tomorrow; spending the whole of Glastonbury Festival panicking about the rain.

The past and the future don't have to dictate your life or cloud your judgement. Mindfulness helps you to become more focused on the life you are living now rather than the life you want to live or the life you should have lived in the past.

Dangerous minds

The first step to becoming more mindful is to try to understand what your mind's up to. You may think that because it's *your* mind, you know all about it, but you don't. Sorry.

Your mind is constantly whirring away, making up versions of events that it presents to you convincingly. In Tom's example (see pages 14–15), his mind presented him with a story that was nonsense – the shops don't always run out of mince whenever he runs in. His mind presented that narrative to him because it was feeding off his mood: frustration and anger. It was trying to help him by finding explanations for his emotions, but it only made things worse.

Example: Alex's pre-emptive panic

Alex worked for a nightmare boss whose main joy in life was to criticise her work. Every time she emailed a report she felt her shoulders creep up around her ears and her back hunch over as she waited for the inevitable storm of passive aggression to sail into her inbox: 'Why haven't you interviewed this person as I asked?'; 'Why haven't you added this section here?'; 'Why did you write this like that?'

Alex knew she was good at her job, yet her boss's constant micro-management was making her question herself. After constantly refreshing her emails for an hour, getting more and more anxious, stressed and angry, she decided to write a draft response in advance, defending her work against the criticisms that she knew were on their way.

And then her boss's email arrived. Alex was in such a state by this point, she couldn't even open it straight away. Instead she sat staring at her computer, feeling unbearably angry, her heart racing and palms sweating. Finally, she took a deep breath, steeled herself and clicked 'open'. It said: 'Great job! Thanks.'

Alex's mind had created a story that fitted her emotions, but it was total fiction. She'd wasted hours stewing over something she thought would happen, but didn't. Our minds do this all the time, chattering along in the background, prodding us to think certain things and behave in certain ways.

Even when you're being mindful, it's inevitable that sometimes you'll still get stressed and upset and follow your mind's advice, but at least you'll be doing it in an informed way. For example, when you're really busy it can be all too easy to cancel social plans, going down the familiar route of thinking, 'I can't be bothered, I just want to watch TV'. You then think up some credible reasons why you can't go: 'I have that early dentist appointment tomorrow, don't I?' However, if you were being mindful, you'd recognise these thoughts for the wily rogues they are. You'd know what they were trying to do and recognise that this happens quite a lot. You could even name them: 'Here are my Excuse Thoughts again' (we discuss naming thoughts more in Chapter 10). Recognising them will allow you to question them: 'Am I really that tired? Don't I normally have a good time when I go?' This will enable you to make an informed choice rather than letting your mind throw you over its shoulder and carry you off down a well-worn path.

Mindfulness teaches you to notice what your mind is doing and to recognise that the stories it tells are just that: stories, not facts. As you become more aware of your thoughts, you'll start to see how much of your unhappiness is caused by the tales you tell yourself. The good news is that those stories can be re-written.

⑤ What's my mind doing right now?
Here's a really simple strategy to get you thinking about stepping back from your mind and seeing it as something separate from your core self – something that can be analysed and considered rather than something that is 100 per cent true and reflective of you as a person.

+ Ask yourself: 'How is my mind right now?' Is it busy? Calm? Are your thoughts racing? Are lots of topics covered in those thoughts? Is it a confusing picture or crystal clear? Have you been concentrating on what you were reading or has your mind wandered off onto other things: shopping, a recent argument, what you're doing later?
+ Acknowledge this moment – that you have stepped back from your thoughts and noted what your mind is doing

Review: Ta-da! It's as simple as that. Just by acknowledging the state of your mind you're starting the mindfulness process. You're becoming more aware. You don't have to change your thoughts or judge them; just be aware of them. As you become more practised, this awareness will allow you to assess thoughts in a more practical way rather than letting them rampage unchecked through your head.

Thoughts in the spotlight

A great way to understand what your mind is doing is to imagine it as a spotlight (one of those huge, old-fashioned theatre lights) focusing your attention on certain objects throughout the day. It's heavy, unwieldy and takes practice and strength to move. Your mind doesn't want to relinquish control, but gradually, with time and practice, you can learn how to make it shine on what you want.

For example, if you're nervous about a speech you've got to give, the spotlight might stubbornly shine on all the previous speeches you've given where you stuttered and stumbled. Or if you're going to a wedding your ex will also be attending, the spotlight will shine on your last argument or all the failures you see in your life since you broke up. With practice, mindfulness will teach you how to swing it to instead shine on the great speeches you've made or on all the good times you shared with your ex and all the great things you've got in your life now.

When should you use mindfulness?

All the time! Mindfulness is something you can practise every single day, whatever your mood or situation, allowing you to get to know yourself better and recognise when you're going down unhelpful paths.

Here are some common mindsets we may all experience that mindfulness helps combat:

+ **Trapped:** feeling as if you're a puppet, with no control over your own life or decisions
+ **Exhausted:** you're sapped of mental and physical energy, just existing rather than living
+ **Unhappy:** you wouldn't class yourself as depressed, but you feel a constant low-level tug of sadness that colours most things you do
+ **Dissatisfied:** something's missing from your life, but you don't know what
+ **Overwhelmed:** there aren't enough hours in the day and you can never catch up with your to-do list
+ **Regretful or resentful:** you can't stop dwelling on past situations or mistakes
+ **Stressed:** you experience stress acutely, both physically and mentally, reacting to real situations (such as an upcoming interview) or imagined ones (such as believing neutral events are negative – 'He's angry at me') in exhausting and unhelpful ways
+ **Depressed or anxious:** see the box on the next page

Mindfulness is proven to help with stress, depression and anxiety, but even if you feel pretty great in general it's a wonderful skill to have in your toolkit, teaching you how to get the most out of life.

We can't stop stressful, upsetting or traumatic things from occurring in our lives. Shit happens: it's unavoidable. Whether the issue is temporary (like when your car breaks down) or whether it's more long-term (such as dealing with a family member who's very ill) life can kick you in the teeth. Even the things that are positive and exciting – a wedding, having a baby, getting a new job – can induce hair-pulling stress. With so much going on,

Depression and anxiety

Depression and anxiety are classed as mental health problems and sadly the number of people affected by them is on the rise, with one in four people in the UK experiencing some kind of mental health issue in the course of a year.

Symptoms of depression

Depression affects your emotions, thoughts, behaviour and body. It can creep up on you out of nowhere or stem from a specific event or trauma. Clinical manuals characterise depression as 'an alteration from previous functioning' – such as a change for the worse in how you're behaving and feeling. Sufferers will experience five or more of the following symptoms during a two-week period (one of which must be low mood or diminished interest or pleasure. It's also important to rule out whether the symptoms could result from a mind-altering substance or general medical condition):

+ Low mood
+ Diminished interest or pleasure
+ Change to appetite
+ Lack of sleep
+ Purposeless motions such as pacing, hand-wringing or excessive fidgeting
+ Fatigue or loss of energy
+ Feelings of worthlessness or excessive or inappropriate guilt
+ Diminished ability to think or concentrate
+ Recurrent thoughts of death or suicide

Symptoms of anxiety

We all experience feelings of anxiety from time to time – it's a natural response to a perceived threat to either your physical or psychological wellbeing, such as a car being driven straight at you (physical) or being made redundant (psychological). Situations like this can trigger your in-built fight or flight response (a leftover from our cave-dwelling days), which helps you assess risk and keeps you alert. However, anxiety becomes a problem when you're experiencing it all the time and/or when things don't warrant it.

Emotional symptoms include:
+ Feelings of dread, panic or impending doom
+ Feeling on edge and hyper-alert
+ Difficulty sleeping
+ Difficulty concentrating
+ Feelings of being 'trapped' and wanting to escape

Physical symptoms include:
+ Sweating
+ Heavy or fast breathing
+ Hot flushes or blushing
+ Dry mouth
+ Shaking
+ Racing heart
+ Dizziness and fainting
+ Stomach aches and sickness

If you experience any of the above symptoms regularly it's important to see your GP and get checked out, in case you need more specialist help. However, this book will also help by making you more aware of negative patterns and teaching you how to stop ruminating on the past and worrying about the future.

it can be easy to focus on your angst and lose perspective on life as a whole. Mindfulness is a way of paying attention to both the good and the bad in your life in more productive ways. So, yes, your boiler might break down or you might hate your job; you might lose someone close to you or spill red wine on your mother-in-law's sofa; you might go through a relationship break-up or have money troubles. Such things are all stressful in different measures, but you can cope, despite what your thoughts may tell you. Learning to stop your mind spiralling out of control when you come up against tough events will make life infinitely calmer.

We, as humans, have been designed to feel the full spectrum of emotions – everything from table-dancing euphoria to hide-in-bed sorrow – and that's something to be celebrated. You wouldn't know joy if you never experienced sadness. Our emotions are our way of processing events in our lives appropriately so we can then move on. Without stress, anxiety, anger or sadness we'd be robots. Mindfulness will teach you how to focus on the present and deal with your emotions – whatever they are – effectively, so you can live a fulfilling, happy and peaceful life.

⑤ Why am I interested in becoming more mindful?

Write down in your notebook reasons why you were drawn to this book. What is it about mindfulness that's attractive to you? Why would you like to become more mindful? Here are some suggestions that may strike a chord:

+ I feel I'm missing out on life; that life's passing me by
+ I want to deal with stress better
+ I'd like to feel more in control
+ I want to be more present and enjoy life more
+ Sometimes I react to things badly and act out in certain ways. I'd like to be able to curb this behaviour

Review: Did some of your reasons take you by surprise? Often we start things on what seems to be a whim, when we're actually being driven by deeper desires, fears or motivations. By writing down your reasons you'll be more inclined to take mindfulness seriously. If you hit a lull, you can return to this list and remind yourself why you started the process and what you hope to achieve.

Thoughts to take away

✓ Mindfulness will enable you to live in the moment, so life doesn't pass you by

✓ Mindfulness will teach you to deal with stressful situations calmly so you feel more in control

✓ You'll acknowledge your moods and thoughts as transient 'events' that come and go, accepting that they don't define who you are and don't have to dictate what you do

2

Mindfulness-based Cognitive Therapy

The most commonly practised version of mindfulness is mindfulness-based cognitive therapy (MBCT). This chapter explains how it works and how it can help you.

What is mindfulness-based cognitive therapy?

The words 'mindfulness-based cognitive therapy' (MBCT) may conjure up images of wild-haired scientists prodding brains in jars, but it's absolutely nothing of the sort. MBCT is just a fancy name for the most commonly practised version of mindfulness, which forms the basis of this book.

A bit of history: Dr Jon Kabat-Zinn first introduced mindfulness into a healthcare setting in 1979 as a way to help people learn to live with chronic medical conditions. He and his colleagues developed an eight-week mindfulness-based stress reduction (MBSR) programme of meditative exercises focused on developing patience, compassion and acceptance so that the participants' disabilities wouldn't dominate and dictate their lives.

Psychologists in the UK and Canada developed the programme further, combining mindfulness with cognitive therapy (MBCT). Cognitive therapy is one of the leading problem-focused treatments for a broad variety of disorders. Fundamentally it's based on the belief that the way you interpret a situation will influence how you feel emotionally and physically and how you behave. That is: it's not what happens to you that affects you, it's how you evaluate what happens.

We've illustrated what we mean in a simple diagram called a mind map (see opposite – they'll get more interesting as we go on, promise). It shows how your thoughts (your interpretations and evaluations of an event), body (physicality), behaviour and emotions are all connected.

Where mindfulness comes in (where cognitive therapy becomes mindfulness-based cognitive therapy) is learning to become more aware, moment by moment, of your thoughts, body, mood and behaviour so you can stop habitual negative patterns. Still with us? Hope so. The example opposite will help explain things.

Physicality
How did your body react?
(sweatiness, tension,
racing heart)

Thoughts
What went through your
mind during/immediately
after the event?

Event
What happened?

Behaviour
What did you do or have
an impulse or urge to do?

Emotions
How did you feel? (sad,
angry, defensive)

Example: Gemma's bad joke

Gemma tagged along with her friend Clare to a birthday party, where she
didn't know many people, promising herself (and Clare) that she'd be the
perfect guest. Clare went to get them some drinks while Gemma joined a
group of people. Trying to catch up with the conversation, Gemma heard
someone mentioning the name of a man Clare worked with who Clare wasn't
particularly fond of. Gemma, keen to fit in and make people laugh, made a
joke about the guy's infamous bad breath and everyone went quiet, ...∴.

⋯⋯ looking a mixture of horrified and awkward. Gemma's heart sank into her shoes. Panicking, she left the party in a hurry, without even saying goodbye to Clare. She couldn't face telling her friend that she'd made an awful faux pas and probably landed her in trouble.

When Clare rang her several times later, Gemma was too ashamed and embarrassed to pick up. The next day she sent her a curt text telling her she'd left because she felt ill. Clare stopped trying to get hold of her after a couple of days and they didn't speak for over a week.

Gemma's mind map
looked like this:

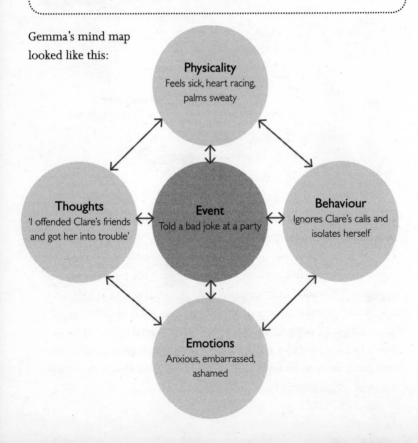

Physicality
Feels sick, heart racing,
palms sweaty

Thoughts
'I offended Clare's friends
and got her into trouble'

Event
Told a bad joke at a party

Behaviour
Ignores Clare's calls and
isolates herself

Emotions
Anxious, embarrassed,
ashamed

How Gemma interpreted the situation – that she'd made a terrible joke, landed her friend in trouble and insulted other guests – affected her mood, body and behaviour, causing a vicious circle of stress, anxiety and negativity – each stage feeding the next.

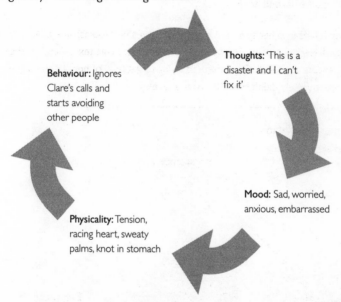

Thoughts: 'This is a disaster and I can't fix it'

Mood: Sad, worried, anxious, embarrassed

Physicality: Tension, racing heart, sweaty palms, knot in stomach

Behaviour: Ignores Clare's calls and starts avoiding other people

This kind of negativity can snowball, triggering habitual pessimistic thoughts (for example, 'This is a disaster and I can't fix it') and actions (for example, hiding away, avoiding the issue). In Gemma's case, by ignoring Clare she doesn't give herself a chance to disprove her fears so they only get worse: 'I offended Clare's friends and got her into trouble' quickly becomes 'She'll tell everyone what I did and they'll all think I'm an idiot'. Before long she's not even thinking about the original event – that she made a bad joke – she's thinking about how she's an awful person who deserves to have lost all her friends! She's raced so far down the wrong path she's lost all sense of perspective.

If Gemma had been practising mindfulness she would have been able to step back from those thoughts and seen them for what they were – simply thoughts, not facts; just her mind's version of events, not the definitive version of events. She then would have had a choice as to whether she wanted to believe her mind's story (that her life was over because of a joke) or whether there might be another view. She could then have spoken to Clare to find out what actually happened. They probably would have had a good laugh about it.

By practising mindfulness Gemma's mind map would have looked like this:

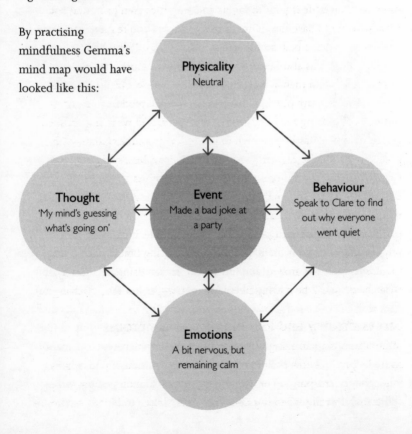

Physicality
Neutral

Thought
'My mind's guessing what's going on'

Event
Made a bad joke at a party

Behaviour
Speak to Clare to find out why everyone went quiet

Emotions
A bit nervous, but remaining calm

Why mindfulness is great

As Gemma's example hopefully illustrated, mindfulness will make you feel more in control of your mood and thoughts, leaving you better able to cope with whatever life throws at you. Research shows that over time, practising mindfulness meditations increases levels of happiness and feelings of wellbeing and fulfilment long-term. People who practise regularly report feeling less anxious, stressed, depressed, exhausted or irritable – which makes sense. Of course, you're going to live a happier, more contented life if your thoughts and emotions aren't running riot. How amazing to have the ability to recognise that you're careering down a well-worn negative path so you can stop and go a different, better way.

Mindfulness has also been proven to improve memory, creativity, reaction times and mental and physical stamina. How? Because you're present. You're aware of what's happening, not just plodding or racing through life waiting for some kind of revelation. And we're not finished yet: mindfulness has been shown to bolster the immune system, with people who practise regularly visiting their doctor less, spending fewer days in hospital and suffering less from chronic stress and hypertension. Clinical trials have shown that meditating halves the risk of experiencing recurring depression; it can reduce the mental strain of chronic physical pain and even relieve drug and alcohol dependence. It can even have a physical effect on your brain, positively influencing brain patterns that underlie day-to-day anxiety and low mood. So practising isn't just a life-style choice, you'll be making physiological changes too. It's powerful stuff.

Stress, anxiety and low mood: the symptoms

Mindfulness is an amazing way to combat stress, anxiety and low mood, so it's helpful to know how to recognise those emotions and thoughts when they're creeping up on you. (More often than not we only realise something's wrong when our nails are already bitten to bloody stumps or we're halfway through a bottle of gin.) On the next couple of pages we've listed the most common symptoms of stress, anxiety and low mood. Running through the list may seem intimidating, but you can't feel differently if you don't recognise how you feel in the first place.

Some points on the list will be familiar to you, but others might be more surprising. If you're an angry person, you might think, 'That's just the way I am' rather than realising that anger can be a result of stress. It's the same with people who class themselves as 'worriers' or 'pessimists' believing they're 'just made that way'. Nope, those feelings are caused by something, so why not look for the triggers so you can make changes?

We all – all – experience stress, anxiety and low mood and while individual responses vary they're along the same lines. You might become withdrawn and not engage with others, trying to avoid situations that could provoke more stress. Or you might seek reassurance from others. Alternatively you might become hyper and try to do everything all at once, blitzing through your days to avoid thinking about underlying issues or desperately trying to keep on top of responsibilities. We're all different, but these reactions are normal, so don't ever feel alone. This is an exercise in getting to know yourself better, so tick off the symptoms that apply to you.

Emotions

- ❑ Anxious
- ❑ Low
- ❑ Frustrated
- ❑ Angry
- ❑ Sensitive
- ❑ Defensive
- ❑ Irritable
- ❑ Depressed
- ❑ Fearful
- ❑ Ashamed
- ❑ Insecure
- ❑ Panicky
- ❑ Guilty
- ❑ Restless
- ❑ Numb/empty
- ❑ Helpless
- ❑ Impatient
- ❑ Frightened
- ❑ Distracted

Physicality

- ❑ General tension, aches and pains
- ❑ Muscular cramps and spasms
- ❑ Nervous twitches
- ❑ Increased heart rate
- ❑ Constipation or diarrhoea
- ❑ Churning stomach
- ❑ Nausea
- ❑ Dizziness
- ❑ Fainting
- ❑ Pins and needles
- ❑ Difficulty swallowing
- ❑ Tearfulness
- ❑ Insomnia
- ❑ Feeling sluggish or restless

⋯⋱

❑ Increased or decreased appetite
❑ Sweating
❑ Breathlessness
❑ Exhaustion
❑ Spot outbreaks/skin irritations
❑ Loss of libido
❑ Tendency to contract colds and infections

Thoughts

❑ Worries about the future ('What if…?')
❑ Self-focused ('The whole world's out to get me'/'Why does this always happen to me?')
❑ Self-blaming ('This is my fault'/'I always mess things up')
❑ Comparative ('She wouldn't have messed this up')
❑ Catastrophising/fearing the worst ('This is going to be a disaster')
❑ Doubting your ability to cope ('I can't handle this')
❑ Taking things personally ('They're talking about me')
❑ Ruminating (dwelling on things in the past)
❑ Racing (vague/unstructured/unconnected thoughts)
❑ Insecure ('I'm not good enough'/'I'm a fraud')
❑ Bleak, despairing or mournful ('Nothing will ever get better')

Behaviour

- ❑ Increased drinking/smoking/drug-taking
- ❑ Over- or under-eating
- ❑ Withdrawing from life/stopping pleasurable activities
- ❑ Procrastinating
- ❑ Nail-biting
- ❑ Snapping at people
- ❑ Poor time management
- ❑ Being distracted/not concentrating
- ❑ Difficulty making decisions
- ❑ Being accident-prone/clumsy
- ❑ Becoming a workaholic
- ❑ Absenteeism (both professionally and socially)
- ❑ Not looking after yourself physically
- ❑ Becoming reckless
- ❑ Hyper/always in a rush (this can include talking more and faster)
- ❑ Forgetfulness (e.g. forgetting your keys/to lock up/call someone)
- ❑ Constantly seeking reassurance

⑤ Your own mind map

Now you've identified some of your key stressed-out thoughts, emotions, physicality and behaviour fill in your own mind map to start seeing for yourself how they're all connected (see right).

A good place to start is to think of a recent time when you summarised how you felt in one word: 'I feel terrible'; 'That was a disaster'; 'Everything is rubbish'; 'This is so unfair'. Often we condense an entire experience into one word, but no matter how satisfying it sounds to shout out loud, one word is never going to represent what you're going through. However, we all do it and it's an easy place to start, so think of the last time you spluttered out an adjective in sadness, fury, embarrassment or exasperation and fill in your own mind map using that as the starting point under 'thoughts'. Then remember how your body felt, your mood and what you did or felt an impulse to do.

If nothing springs to mind, think of the last time you felt anxiety physically (for example when your heart pounded) and work from there. Or, think of something you did that was out of character. Perhaps you threw something, snapped at someone or wrote an angry email. What prompted that behaviour? Use any section as a starting point and fill in the gaps.

An example of what your own mind map might be like:

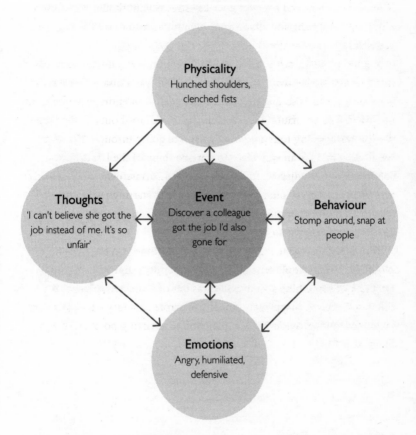

Physicality
Hunched shoulders,
clenched fists

Thoughts
'I can't believe she got the
job instead of me. It's so
unfair'

Event
Discover a colleague
got the job I'd also
gone for

Behaviour
Stomp around, snap at
people

Emotions
Angry, humiliated,
defensive

Review: Working through the mind map will give you the chance to make changes. Each section offers an intervention point – an opportunity to become aware of habitual negative patterns or vicious circles. It should also raise red flags over using emotive words or phrases and accepting them as facts. In the example in the mind map, thinking 'it's so unfair' triggers thoughts along the lines that the person who got the job didn't deserve it and that nothing ever goes right for you. Both interpretations will leave you feeling resentful, bitter and angry. The word 'unfair' probably whizzed into your head without you realising it's an emotional ticking time bomb. By filling in the mind map you should start to see the stories your mind is telling you and the negative impact these words have.

What happens now?

Mindfulness teaches you to become more aware of the subtle ways your mind influences your behaviour, so you can make informed decisions about how you want to act, rather than blundering on mindlessly. By stepping back and taking a more level-headed view events won't evoke the same levels of distress.

When you practise mindfulness, you deliberately turn your attention to your thoughts, emotions and physical feelings as they happen. You can then learn to recognise them for what they are – transient reactions provoked by each other and the context – and then you can decide what action you want to take, if any. You'll also become more adept at noticing when your mind flings obstacles in your way, finding ways to navigate them. By living this way you'll always see the bigger picture and avoid getting caught up in negative and destructive spirals.

Remember: thoughts are just thoughts and feelings are just feelings – they are what they are and not a definition of who you are. Accepting this is a big step in becoming more mindful. You can start to see the chatter of stress, unhappiness or annoyance as background noise, radio static that you can turn down. Or, if you want a more visual representation, see those thoughts as black clouds in the sky: they're definitely there, but you and they are separate entities and you can choose how to react to them. You can either climb into the black cloud, letting it smother you, or watch it with a friendly curiosity until it drifts away.

You are in control. Realising you have a choice in how and whether you act on your thoughts and feelings is very liberating.

This book will teach you to:

1 Recognise that your thoughts, mood, body and behaviour are all connected
2 Identify moods, thoughts and physical reactions through mindfulness
3 Realise that your thoughts and feelings don't have to control you – you can choose how to react to them

Thoughts to take away

✓ Your thoughts, mood, body and behaviour are all connected and all offer ways to make changes

✓ Understanding how you personally respond to stress, anxiety and low mood will make you more aware of habitual negative patterns

✓ Mindfulness will stop knee-jerk reactions to events, making you calmer, happier and more content

3

A State of Mind

Mindfulness pairs up 'formal' meditative and 'informal' everyday practices. Here we explain what they are, why they're important and introduce strategies in both categories.

A mind of your own

The whole point of mindfulness is to learn to live your life more mindfully every day, while you're seeing your friends, working, looking after your family or waiting for the bus. It means being present in the moment, whatever you're doing. Meditation can help you achieve this.

If you've ever been travelling you'll probably understand what we mean by 'living in the moment' and being aware of your thoughts and feelings as they happen. When you're exploring new places, seeing amazing sights, with no time constraints, you might think, 'Yes! This is brilliant. I'm having a great time right now.' You've gone on a trip specifically to experience things, so you're damn well going to fully appreciate them. But why do you have to travel across the world to feel that way? Wouldn't it be brilliant to truly be present in everything you do, so life doesn't pass you by? Going to the post office might not be as scintillating as visiting Machu Picchu, but it doesn't have to be a total drag, either.

In order for you to become more mindful we're going to ask you to practise both 'formally', by setting aside a specific time to try the meditative tasks, and 'informally' during your daily life.

Two examples of 'informal' mindfulness

Here are two things you probably already do mindfully, without even realising that's what you're doing:

+ Competitive sport: If you play any form of competitive sport you'll have to be mindful while you do it. You can't compete well or play in a team while planning your wedding speech or your next holiday. You have to think about where, what and how you're going to move, what your team mates or competitors are doing and who's got the upper hand. You are completely present in the moment. ⋯⋯⋮⟩

◆ Following a complicated recipe: Timing is key to good cooking so yes, while your mind can wander if you're making beans on toast, it can't wander if you're putting the finishing touches to a Michelin-star-worthy coq au vin. With four pots on the stove, the oven on, steam in your face and a timer ringing it's near-enough impossible to be anything but mindful when dabbling in a bit of cheffing.

If you ask keen sports people or cooks why they love what they do, often they'll say it's because they're completely absorbed in it – it takes their mind off everything else. Being completely focused on what you're doing and how you're feeling will make pleasurable things more enjoyable, boring things less boring and stressful things less distressing.

Formal and informal mindfulness exercises are intrinsically linked – the more formal practices you do the better you'll get at the informal day-to-day stuff. It's time to lower those sceptical eyebrows and prepare to do some meditation.

Formal mindfulness meditations

'Formal' isn't a great word. It conjures up images of silent, serious types who haven't cracked a smile in decades, but it's what this kind of mindfulness is known as generally, so we're going with it.

Formal mindfulness starts with your breathing, focusing on the physical sensations that arise when you exhale and inhale. This is then followed by widening your focus to become aware of sounds, sensations around you and your thoughts and feelings, employing all of your senses. Each strategy will focus on a particular experience (physical, emotional or thoughtful).

Formal strategies can last for anything from 1 minute to several hours. The strategies in this book are between 1 and 20 minutes long. For every strategy we suggest you set a timer to signal the designated time, ensuring the alarm at the end is a relaxing sound (nothing ends a peaceful mood like a fog horn in your ear).

It's helpful to be able to listen to the instructions as you go along rather than having to keep returning to the book. You can record yourself using the book as a script or find similar downloadable exercises on free internet sites such as: www.freemindfulness.org and www.franticworld.com/free-meditations-from-mindfulness. There are also lots of freely available videos on YouTube.

Formal strategies will make you better at informal mindfulness as you'll become more used to tuning in to what's happening within and around you. You'll learn how to notice your thinking patterns and when you start heading down destructive or unhelpful paths. You'll be able to identify your moods and see how they connect to your thoughts, body and behaviour and you'll be able to spot bad habits that end up dictating your day.

Being compassionate, curious and non-judgemental

The word 'compassion' comes up a lot in mindfulness: 'acknowledge your thoughts with compassion and without judgement' is a popular refrain. What this means, quite simply, is to be kinder, warmer and non-judgemental to yourself in numerous ways:

✦ Be curious: if your mind wanders, bring it gently back without getting frustrated – it's just doing what it's used to doing, so don't get angry with it

✦ Try not to be sceptical about what you're doing – mindfulness works!

✦ Congratulate yourself for having a go and remember that mindfulness is a skill that has to be learned; you're not going to master it immediately

✦ Don't judge yourself: there's no right or wrong with mindfulness. You can't 'win' at it, so stop telling yourself you're doing it badly or messing things up

At the end of each strategy we'll ask you some questions about how it went. Please don't ignore these as reflecting on how you felt and what you noticed is an important part of mindfulness (and an important skill when you're learning anything new). There's no point thinking, 'I hated that' and throwing the book out the window without assessing why. That would be like playing tennis for the first time and smashing your racquet to bits if you hit the ball into the net.

Remember: Bad feelings and thoughts pass

The strategies will ask you to 'turn towards' negative feelings, which is probably the opposite of what you normally do, your natural instinct being to run away from them or try to ignore them. Mindfulness is all about learning that feelings are transient – they come and go. Running away, ignoring or indulging in terrible thoughts and feelings (wallowing in them) will only make them worse. Remember the cloud analogy (see page 40)? Well, it's true: your bad mood is there, but it will pass if you allow it to. Remind yourself that you've felt both sad and happy before and you will again.

Some people find that when they start practising mindfulness emotions become more intense. If this happens to you, remember you're not alone and that this is a common experience. You might even take it as a sign that the strategy you're doing is important.

How to go about formal practice

This is the position we recommend you adopt for all formal strategies in the book:

+ Sit up straight on a chair (your spine shouldn't touch the back)
+ Keep your legs uncrossed, your feet flat on the floor
+ Your shoulders and arms should be relaxed, your hands wherever they feel most comfortable

✦ Keep your head up, with your chin slightly dipped
✦ You can have your eyes open or closed. If you keep your eyes open let your gaze fall unfocused onto the floor a few feet in front of you

Of course, if you'd feel more comfortable lying down that's fine, as is sitting cross-legged. Whatever works for you. Turn off your phone, the radio, your computer or any other possible distractions. Close the door and make sure others know not to disturb you. (Consider practising first thing in the morning before the world crashes in.)

A funny thing about time

Put aside twenty minutes every day to practise. Yes, every day. This is the only way to get into a routine that you might actually stick to. One of the most common excuses people come up with is not having enough time to meditate. Yes, you've got a crazy job, two kids, a demanding partner, a limping dog and a leaky roof, but what about the twenty minutes you kept hitting snooze on your alarm this morning or the twenty minutes you spent watching videos of cats wearing hats on YouTube?

You can find time – if you think this is important enough you will – and once you have you'll be gobsmacked at how much extra time you have in general. As we mentioned in Chapter 1, meditation will actually save you time in the long run. There's an old saying that if you have two days to write a letter you'll take two days to write it. You'll ponder what paper to write it on, what pen to use, whether to say 'to' or 'dear'. You'll pace back and forth trying to think of a wonderful first line. You'll fill every single available hour writing that letter. Or you'll put it off until the last possible moment, feeling guilty about your procrastination for two whole days. It'll lurk at the back of your mind, overshadowing everything you do. You'll then scribble something down in five minutes before it's too late. Either way, the whole two days has been spent thinking about, writing or avoiding the letter. Mindfulness focuses your mind to such a degree on the here and now that it will make you unrecognisably productive. Because you're not worrying about the future, regretting the past or procrastinating to an award-wining level you'll actually get stuff done. So, no matter how busy you are, or think you are, please try to put aside twenty minutes a day and stick to it.

⑤ Write down when you're going to practise in your diary
Schedule in when you're going to practise. Actually physically writing it down will make it more 'official' in your head and you'll be less inclined to skip it. Also, note down any potential obstacles that might get in the way and work around them. For example, if someone's due to come over at 9am tomorrow and you're scheduled to start your meditation at 8.30am, start the practice earlier or ask your housemate/partner/kids to make sure they're around to open the door.

We've made this an official strategy because it's massively important. It's all too easy to think, 'I'll start tomorrow' and before you know it a month has passed and not only are you still dealing with all the stress and bother you were before, but you also feel guilty about procrastinating over this.

Remember: you can't 'win' at mindfulness
Please re-read this before every new exercise:
There is no 'right' or 'wrong' with mindfulness – you can't 'win' at it. It's not about success or failure and there's no one-size-fits-all. You're not meant to experience one particular thing or 'see the light'. There's no goal you're meant to be striving towards or perfect mindfulness experience. You're just meant to experience the moment as it is. If you set a goal you'll find yourself constantly measuring how near or far you are from reaching it – an impossible task when it comes to matters of the mind. If you say, 'I will be completely mindful within two weeks' your focus on success will

block your mind from the task itself, which is just to 'be'.

Don't try too hard. Constantly thinking, 'Am I doing this right?', 'Am I messing up?' will make you frustrated and annoyed. It's like cooking a soufflé. If you keep opening the oven door to check that it's rising, it'll sink. The action of checking alters the outcome. Even professional chefs make rubbish soufflés occasionally, so it's pointless to go into this with a grand plan. **Yes, we're basically telling you to start this with no expectations, targets or guarantees** – but that's what mindfulness is all about: acceptance and a complete lack of judgement. Focus on what you're doing, try to trust in the process and see where it takes you. Let your experience be the experience.

If you've never practised meditation before, it can feel very weird and that can be off-putting. Humans are creatures of habit and new things can be frightening. We live in a world where no one wants to look stupid and we have a tendency to feel self-conscious if we're doing anything 'different'. On top of this we live in a manic everything-was-meant-to-be-done-yesterday society, where we pride ourselves on squeezing as much as we can into the smallest possible timeframe. In this environment meditation can be totally alien because you'll feel as if you're not doing anything. 'How dare you just sit there?' your mind will scream. Well, ignore it. It may feel as if meditation isn't a match for the level of stress in your life, but stick with it. It will be doing wonders for your mind and body. Yes, some of the strategies might seem boring, but that doesn't mean you're doing it wrong (because there is no 'wrong'); it just means you should bring your mind back to the task and try again.

Ⓢ The arm test

Try this: run your index finger from your wrist to the inside of your elbow, over and over again, for one minute (set your timer). Concentrate on the physical feeling of your finger running gently down your arm.

Review: What did you notice? How did it feel physically – did it tingle? Did the tingle get stronger over time? Did it start feeling uncomfortable? What was your mind doing? Did you judge yourself, thinking, 'I must look like an idiot'? Did your mind wander off? Did you start thinking about other things? What things?

> ### Example: Kate's first attempt at meditation
>
> Kate did the arm-test strategy for the first time and was surprised at how sensitive her arm felt; it tingled every time she ran her finger down it. Even after she stopped, she noticed the sensation continuing for some time afterwards. As she was doing the exercise she noticed that she thought, 'I've no idea why I'm doing this is and I'm probably not even doing it right'. Her mind then drifted to her evening plans. The timer went off and she suddenly remembered where she was and what she was doing.

Never mind your wandering thoughts

Don't get angry at yourself if your mind wanders, like Kate's did, when you're doing these exercises. The aim is not to stop it wandering, but to notice when it does and bring it back gently to what you're doing. This is one of the very first steps of mindfulness – becoming aware of your mind and what it's doing. You're not trying to clear your mind or empty it out; you're just observing it and beginning to notice common patterns.

Many people complain that their mind's too busy to meditate, that they can't connect with what's going on because their thoughts keep crashing in. They see the fact that their mind continues chattering on in the background as a failure. It's not! Your mind is designed to chatter – that's its entire reason for being. You can't shut it off. What you can do is notice what it's chattering about and then bring your mind back to the task at hand, whether that's a formal strategy, writing an email or chatting on the phone to your gran. Every single time you notice and bring your mind back to the present you're being mindful.

A few things that mindfulness is NOT

We've covered what mindfulness is, but it's also worth running through some of the things it most certainly isn't.

+ It's not about 'winning'. Mindfulness is simply a way to rebalance your life and everyone gets something different from it
+ It will not deaden your mind. Quite the contrary – your mind will never have felt so alive, enabling you to make conscious choices as you respond in the moment
+ Mindfulness is not about relaxation. You might become more relaxed through meditation, but you're not doing it to achieve a state of mind, you're doing it to acknowledge your own state of mind as it is
+ Mindfulness is not about clearing or emptying your mind, it's about noticing what's happening in there
+ A wandering mind is not a bad thing
+ Mindfulness will not turn you into a good person, it will simply give you more informed choices about how you want to behave
+ Practising mindfulness doesn't mean you don't care about the past or the future. It's about seeing the world with greater clarity, so you can take wiser action to change the things that need to be changed

A breath of fresh air

Breathing is at the core of all the mindfulness exercises we'll be recommending. There are several reasons why:

> ⋯⋰
> 1 Breathing takes place in the present – you are breathing right now
>   – therefore focusing on it helps to ground you in the here and now,
>   eliminating the power of rumination and worry.
> 2 Breathing is constant. You are always breathing (hopefully, unless
>   something's gone drastically wrong) and so your breath is always available
>   as something to focus on.
> 3 Breathing is automatic. Your lungs do their job without any interference
>   from you. You can't just choose to stop breathing, just as you can't choose
>   to stop sleeping. This means focusing on it will relieve your mind of its goal-
>   driven preoccupations.
> 4 Breathing is simple. Our lives are complicated, so fixating on your breath is
>   an easy way to stay in the present without long-winded self-analysis.
> 5 Learning to focus on your breath is mindfulness at its most basic and
>   effective. By consciously choosing to focus on your breathing you're getting
>   distance from your thoughts and feelings, thus avoiding slipping into habitual
>   negative cycles.

🅢 Breathing mindfully (part 1)

For the next two minutes (set your timer) simply focus all your attention
on your breath as it enters and leaves your body. If it helps, you can say to
yourself (in your head):

> 'Breathing in, I know that I am breathing in.
> Breathing out, I know that I am breathing out.'

Alternatively you can substitute this for counting, following the rule that
an inhale and exhale are one breath. For example, as you breathe in count
'one' in your head and then as you breathe out count 'one' again. Breathe
in a second time and count 'two'. Breathe out a second time and count

'two'. Continue through to ten, and then return to one again until your timer sounds. If you lose count, just return to one and start again (without chastising yourself for losing count – remember you can't 'win', so losing count doesn't matter).

If you can't get your head around this, just try paying attention to what one breath feels like (an inhale and exhale). Notice the physical sensations of one breath flowing into and out from your body – what happens to your nostrils, your shoulders and your rib cage as you inhale and exhale?

Review: How did you find the exercises? What thoughts, feelings, physical sensations or external distractions did you notice?

We suggested counting or saying 'I know that I am breathing in' as you went along as a way to try to ensure your mind focused on the task. However, chances are (more than likely) that your mind wandered anyway during the 2 minutes and you quickly forgot what you were saying in your head or lost count, right? Don't worry, your job is to start noticing when it wanders, register where it's wandered to and then gently bring it back. Practise until you don't lose count and then you'll be at a stage where you don't need to count at all, but can focus solely on the breath for the full two minutes.

Example: Jenny's breathing difficulties

Jenny tried the exercise and managed to reach the first set of ten breaths without losing count, but then the thought 'What's the point?' pinged into her mind, which led to 'How is this helping with my relationship problems?' She started musing on the issues she was having with her boyfriend and before she knew it the timer went off and she was feeling as riled up and stressed as she had when she started – only now with anger at not having completed the task 'properly' added into the mix.

Jenny's mind map looked like t...

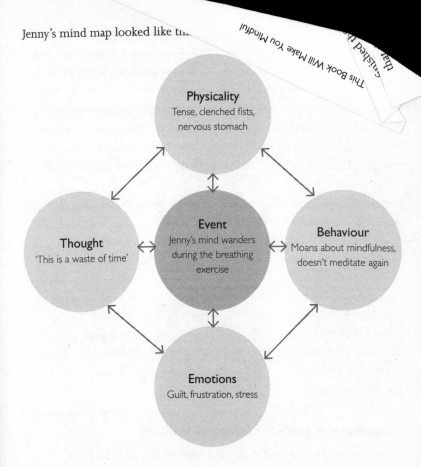

It's easy to get caught up in your thoughts and judgements. We all do it, playing out and reliving arguments and irritations – but it's only making you feel worse. It's important to remember that you're far more likely to be able to deal with the problems and issues in your life if you're feeling calm and level-headed. Mindfulness can give you that. By getting worked up you're only adding to your problems, not solving them. If Jenny strategy and acknowledged that her thoughts did wander, but this was natural and she hadn't 'failed' the task, she would feel more inclined to try again. By acknowledging this progress, the next time she tried she'd be able to bring her mind back to the task when her thoughts interrupted again rather than following them down a negative path.

Jenny's more mindful mind map:

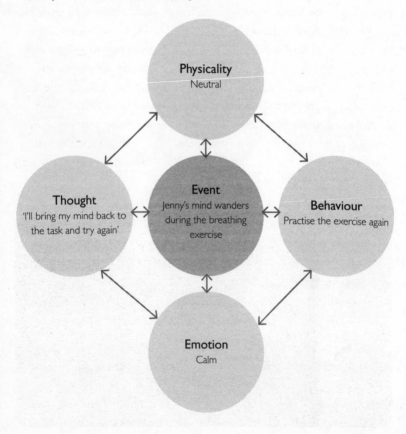

This strategy is one of the first steps in recognising your thoughts for what they are, without indulging them or getting swept up in them: something you'll start doing more in your day-to-day life when you get more confident at formal practices.

Don't give up

Even though you might agree with the theory of mindfulness in principle and be totally open-minded about how it could work for you, it's still hard. Your mind may wander into areas you don't want it to go, you may feel restless and you may think you're wasting valuable time when you could be out doing something. Some days you may feel as if you've got it nailed and others you may feel you're back to where you started. These responses are totally normal, but trust us – you are doing amazing things, even if it doesn't feel like it: you're learning how your mind works and how to separate yourself from its wily clutches. Keep at it and you'll soon realise you're being more mindful day-to-day.

Thoughts to take away

✓ Formal mindfulness (meditative exercises) will aid informal mindfulness (being present in your day-to-day life). Both are as important as each other

✓ You can't 'win' at mindfulness, so be patient and keep practising

✓ It's normal for your mind to wander. Just noticing it has, and bringing it back to the present, is being mindful

4

Mind Games

Does it often seem your mind tells you angst-inducing stories and dredges up painful memories just to torment you? This chapter will teach you how to recognise and therefore win at mind games.

How your mind works

Most people go about their daily lives giving their mind free rein to do whatever it wants, not realising they can *choose* what to focus on. Fingers crossed, you're starting to tune into your thoughts and can see how taking a step back will help you to get a fairer view of what's happening. A key part of mindfulness is to understand why your mind does what it does, so you can recognise when it's being crafty, mean, ludicrous or downright rude.

At the moment your mind is like an untrained puppy. A cute one with big winsome eyes. It bounds about, digs up the flower beds, bites the postman and chews up your brand-new shoes. Now, whether you like dogs or not is irrelevant; you have been put in charge of this puppy and you have to try to train it. You start slowly and eventually it learns to come when you call. Then to sit. Then to roll over. Eventually it stops digging up the flower beds and only bites the postman occasionally. The thing is, though, it's still a puppy. It still runs off sometimes and gets rowdy. With mindfulness, your mind will still do whatever it pleases, running off on tangents and getting up to all kinds of mischief, but through training, practice and patience, you'll become more understanding and tolerant of both it and yourself.

This chapter will explain four of the key reasons why your mind behaves the way it does:

1 The fight or flight response
2 Memory
3 Senses
4 Upbringing

The fight or flight response

We may dress up in fancy clothes and live out our lives via complicated gadgets, but fundamentally we're just animals. We still have the same ingrained survival instincts that our cavemen and cavewomen ancestors relied upon so heavily and just because we don't have to hide from woolly mammoths to survive any more doesn't mean those primitive instincts have disappeared.

We have an automatic inborn reaction to stress and anxiety called the 'fight or flight response' triggered in a part of our brains called the amygdala by a perception of threat or danger. The amygdala is part of the limbic system, a set of brain structures at the top of the brainstem that process our emotions.

Imagine you're sauntering down the street when suddenly a lion charges at you from out of the bushes. You have two choices: either fight the lion or start sprinting in the opposite direction. Both options will require excessive physical strength and to facilitate this, your sympathetic (and very efficient) nervous system floods your body with adrenaline and cortisol. Your heart starts beating faster, pumping blood away from the places that don't need it to the muscles and limbs that need additional fuel for either running or fighting. These muscles will tense up ready for action. Your respiratory rate increases, forcing more oxygen into your bloodstream and heightening your senses so your pupils dilate to sharpen your sight, your ears turn into hyper-sensitive microphones and your perception of pain diminishes. Blood is diverted away from the skin's surface and your fingers and toes, which can result in paleness, tingling and 'cold feet'. This is so that if the lion swipes you with its claws you're less likely to bleed to death (disgusting, but very clever). You also begin to sweat to keep from overheating.

You're in 'attack mode', prepared, both physically and psychologically, for either fight or flight. Your rational mind has taken a backseat – when faced with a lion you don't have time to think, 'Why the hell is there a lion in the street?' – it's there and now you have to deal with it. Your body knows those type of thoughts will only slow you down, so banishes them. When you feel this way, everything is a potential threat. You'll overreact to the slightest provocation as your sense of fear is at survival pitch. The physical change you've gone through is dramatic. The fact that blood has been diverted away from the bits that don't need it can result in nausea or constipation as your digestive tract shuts down. Also, your saliva glands will stop secreting saliva, resulting in a dry mouth, while your rapid breathing can cause dizziness and hot flushes.

When you've dodged the lion, climbed a tree and called the local zoo, your parasympathetic system kicks in. This means your nerves release noradrenaline, which help to reverse the changes that have taken place, gradually cooling you down and returning everything to normal.

Isn't that whole process spectacular? Well, kind of.

Fight or flight used to be integral for human survival – the difference between life or death. The trouble is, thousands of years later we're still programmed exactly the same. The amygdala can't distinguish between an external threat, like a lion, and an internal psychological one, like an argument or an upcoming job interview. This means your fight or flight reflex can be triggered whenever you feel fear, anxiety or stress – handy for lion-dodging, not so handy when trying to negotiate a salary increase.

Money problems, hideous in-laws and health concerns can't be bested by fighting or running away (actually, we'll reserve judgement on the in-laws). However, your body doesn't know that and prepares you just the same. Adrenaline and cortisol are quick to kick in and all rational thoughts disappear. Noradrenaline is slow to calm you down, meaning physically it can take ages to get over things.

And that's not all. Fight or flight doesn't only happen to real tangible problems, but also to imagined ones, for instance fearing you've embarrassed yourself or being scared of receiving criticism. In our current high-pressure, high-demand culture, the body's stress response is activated so often that sometimes it doesn't have a chance to return to normal, resulting in a state of on-going tension.

When you suffer from recurring stress your body and mind lose their ability to deal with day-to-day realities. Your body's not designed to be in this state constantly and so will start compensating for the energy loss by taking it from other places, like your immune system. You may experience aches and pains, digestive problems, lose your appetite, become run down and find you're more susceptible to illness. You can battle on for a while, but these symptoms can eventually lead to burn-out.

This perpetual state of fight or flight doesn't only happen to people under constant pressure, but also, interestingly, to people who are goal-obsessed and who rush about mindlessly from one task to another. Research has shown that people who class themselves as 'doers' or as 'restless' have an amygdala that is on high alert all the time. In their case, the 'threat' is not achieving what they aim to achieve daily so the 'danger' never passes.

Old brain versus new brain

Professor Paul Gilbert, head of the mental health research unit at the University of Derby, believes that what we have just described is a direct result of our 'old brains'. When our brains first evolved our main concerns were survival-related: to find food, water and shelter and avoid lions. But we also needed to have and maintain a social position within our group. It still mattered whether we had a partner, what our roles were in providing for our children and our relationship to the rest of the people around us. We were motivated by a desire for security and we still fought rejection and criticism with anger, anxiety and defensiveness.

However, as we evolved so did our brains. We became conscious of ourselves in a way other animals aren't. We can plan and reason. We can create, imagine and have faith. We can look back, reflect and, yes, ruminate.

⋯∵ Our amazing brains have made us into the species we are today, but our 'old brains' are still alive and well, meaning we're still slaves to our most basic fears, instincts and desires. We're sensitive to how others perceive us, we still have an in-built drive to 'fit in', we employ 'survival of the fittest' comparisons without even realising it ('I'm better/uglier/cleverer/weaker than him or her') and we fear criticism, embarrassment and rejection. All of these things will register as a 'threat' or 'danger' in our amygdala, triggering fight or flight and sparking a reaction totally different to how we might behave if we were able to employ our 'new brains' and think rationally, logically, creatively and open-mindedly about what's happening.

Thankfully mindfulness can limit the effect of fight or flight by identifying the triggers. You can learn how to recognise the symptoms and so put the brakes on the subsequent negative chain reaction.

Thanks (not so much) for the memories

Both your old brain and new brain have a key weapon in their arsenal when it comes to making you feel anxious, worried or sad: memory. As a human being, your emotions are intrinsically connected to memory. When you're feeling a certain way, your mind will rifle through your memories trying to find one that fits what you're experiencing now. It's pretty clever, actually. It's trying to find a reference point, something that will explain why you're feeling the way you are and what you should do about it. By spotting similarities, your brain can try to find a solution.

When you're feeling great this can be a positive experience. Your mind cherry-picks memories when you felt similar and you'll be bathed in a warm glow of wellbeing. However, when you feel stressed, anxious or unhappy your mind will make you re-live that time you unknowingly chatted up your friend's dad or the time you got fired for accidentally sending an email about your boss to your boss. It's a domino effect, each memory piling on feelings of fear, inadequacy or frustration until you're thinking, 'Nothing ever goes right in my life'.

These self-attacking thoughts are incredibly powerful and once they've got their claws into you they're painfully hard to shift and will affect your body, mood and behaviour.

Example: Louise's lateness bug-bear

Louise was waiting for her friend Emily. Again. Emily was always late. And because she was always late she seemed to think it was OK – that people should just assume she'd be tardy and it wasn't a problem. She usually didn't even apologise when she finally rocked up – it drove Louise mad.

The clock ticked on…and on. By the time Emily was 20 minutes late (with no explanatory text or phone call) Louise was so furious she'd given herself a headache. 'I knew this would happen!' she hissed to herself, her mind flicking over previous times she'd been left waiting. The worst was a few weeks ago when Emily had been over an hour late. 'She obviously doesn't care that I'm sitting here on my own. I bet she doesn't do this to other people. She's probably laughing at me right now! Actually, she does always make me the butt of her jokes, like that time she mocked my haircut. She's actually pretty rude in general – she was obnoxious to my sister that time. That's it, I'm going!' And she stormed out.

Louise's mind map
looked like this:

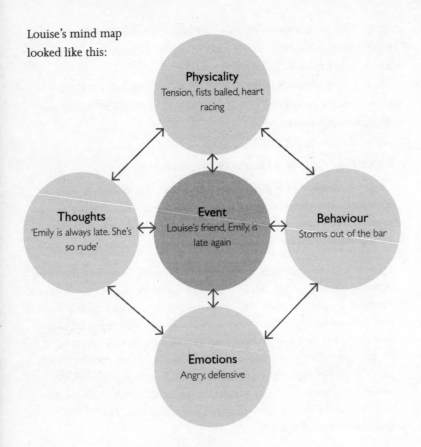

⑤ Your own memory mind map

Think of the last time you had a tiff or full-blown argument with a friend, colleague, family member, child or partner. What triggered your anger? Now try to remember whether your mind conjured up a list of other things they'd done that you could also be mad about. Your mind's memory finder isn't choosy. It'll find any old memories that fit the angry/frustrated/embarrassed bill. As in Louise's case above, instead of just being angry about Emily's lateness her mind dredged up other memories to be upset about too – that she'd laughed at her haircut and was rude to her sister – that had nothing to do with being late.

Fill in a mind map listing both the original reason you were angry and then some of the subsequent thoughts provoked by your memory.

We've filled in another example to help you out:

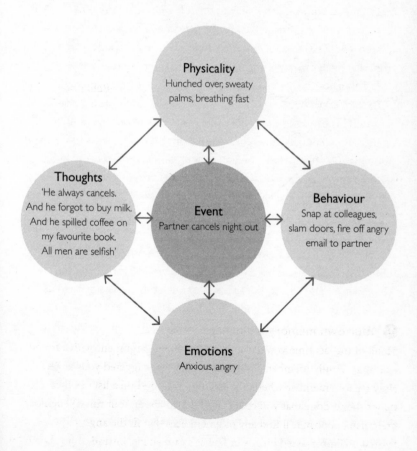

Physicality
Hunched over, sweaty palms, breathing fast

Thoughts
'He always cancels. And he forgot to buy milk. And he spilled coffee on my favourite book. All men are selfish'

Event
Partner cancels night out

Behaviour
Snap at colleagues, slam doors, fire off angry email to partner

Emotions
Anxious, angry

Your mind thinks it's helping out by providing examples of previous times you've felt the same, but it's actually doing the opposite: winding you up even more.

Mindfulness will teach you how to recognise what your mind is doing and to treat these thoughts with the suspicion they deserve, so you can get some distance and consider whether they have any merit. Is your partner cancelling on you really the same as them forgetting to buy milk? Is their behaviour really representative of their gender as a whole? Do you really want to wade into these memories and let them make you feel worse? From there you can work out whether you want to act on these thoughts.

Sensory overload

Your mind is like a big store room filled with row upon row of filing cabinets. Each contains different information that can be unlocked by your emotions and senses. Have you ever caught the smell of someone's perfume and been catapulted back to a teenage party? Or eaten something that made you immediately think of your childhood? Or heard the refrain of a song and been transported back to a summer holiday?

Sights, sounds, tastes, smells and touch can all unlock memories – memories you hadn't even realised you'd stored. You might visit somewhere you haven't been in years and before you arrive you can't remember much about it, but as soon as you get there your senses kick in and the dusty recollections come flooding back.

Your senses can inspire both feelings of nostalgia (fond recollections) and unhappy memories and the triggers can be extremely subtle: a stranger's mobile ringtone on the bus, the smell of someone's shampoo in the queue in front of you, the taste of a hastily bought croissant on the way to work. You're innocently going about your business and then suddenly it's ten years ago and you're kissing someone, whose name escapes you, on a beach.

If you're stressed or anxious and your fight or flight reflex has kicked in, your senses will be on hyper-alert and so will be more sensitive to these external triggers. Have you ever been trying to avoid someone and every single person you pass suddenly looks like them? Or you think you hear their voice everywhere? Your senses are trying to hunt out threats and dangers and will link all of these things together in your mind.

How your upbringing brings things up

The stories your mind tells you and the way you interpret situations will have been influenced by the experiences you had as a child. Your beliefs and impressions of yourself and others are formed and developed in childhood: impressions of self-worth, achievement, acceptance and lovability. When you're a kid you accept what you are told (generally by your parents or those closest to you) as you have no basis for comparison. This will have shaped how you deal with problems, how well you feel you can cope with emotional anguish and how confident you feel within.

If you were given the impression you were an ugly or stupid child, those ideas will have shaped, to a degree, how you feel you measure up as an adult. While rationally you might know you're not ugly or stupid it's become a belief on which other convictions are based. If you always felt you were never quite as bright or academically able as a sibling this may well have influenced your ambitions and ideas around what achievement means and how it's measured. And if your parents were worriers, they may have passed on a tendency to become over-anxious. All of these things can affect your self-esteem and mould your thinking patterns.

People who have had difficult childhoods often find themselves striving for success or to better themselves according to the beliefs that shaped their youth, for example striving for professional success, 'improving' their appearance or fitness levels or trying to be 'cool' socially. However, no matter how much they achieve they'll probably still feel something's missing because they've never dealt with their underlying fears; they'll never reach an acceptable standard in their own heads.

Luckily mindfulness can help with this.

How mindfulness can give you peace of mind

When your mind is reeling and you're about to launch into full-blown fight or flight mode mindfulness will give you the tools to step back, recognise what's happening and in doing so stop the cycle. By simply noticing what your mind is doing ('I'm starting to panic'/ 'I'm freaking out'/ 'I'm getting riled up') you're slowing things down so you won't suddenly find yourself cowering under your desk with no idea how you got there. You're giving yourself a choice: do I mull over this 'threat' and all its possible consequences, pick over the times I've felt this way before, dive headfirst into destructive emotions that will ruin my day OR do I view this threat rationally?

Mindfulness meditation teaches you to recognise damaging thoughts and memories as they arise, acknowledge them and then let them go. By 'let them go' we don't mean ignore the issue or problem, we mean let the whirling, unhelpful thoughts go so that other, more productive, ones can take their place.

One key thing to remember: this isn't about 'positive thinking'. Mindfulness is about acknowledging everything that's happening – the good, the bad and the neutral – so you can better handle bad stuff and likewise more fully enjoy good stuff. By knowing your thoughts are going down a familiar path of panic or anxiety and knowing what tends to follow you can say to yourself: 'memories are just memories – they're in the past. They aren't what's happening now.' Giving yourself that choice is extraordinarily powerful.

Mindfulness breaks the cycle of rumination and worry that keeps the amygdala in the alert position and triggers the fight or flight reflex.

It changes how we perceive an event so we can change our response to it. For example, 'This is a disaster, just like when…' becomes 'This isn't great, but these feelings will pass and I can cope with it'.

Two common arguments against mindfulness

1 'I love that buzzy feeling of always being on the go. I'm firing on all cylinders and getting more done. Why would I want to stop that?'

When you're constantly under pressure it's harder to keep your attention on one thing. You chop and change between jobs so that you aren't ever truly focused on what you're doing. Flitting about gives the impression of busyness, but you're actually achieving less than you would if you really concentrated on each thing. And yes, while a bit of adrenaline can motivate you and get you through a difficult task it's not sustainable long-term. Your body is not built to be constantly aroused in that way; you'll crash and burn at some point.

2 'Pressure, stress and anxiety get me closer to reaching my goals.'

You can still reach your goals and work hard without beating yourself up over past defeats or near-misses. And you will beat yourself up if you're always constantly looking to the future and never appreciating the present. You'll keep moving the goalposts, meaning that nothing you do will be enough. By concentrating on what you're doing day-to-day you'll actually achieve far more, to a better standard and gain more pleasure from doing it.

⑤ Breathing mindfully (part 2)

This strategy builds on the one from the last chapter (see page 53), focusing on 'the length of your breath' as it flows in and out of your body.

◆ Sit down, as specified in Chapter 3 (see page 47), or lie on your back. Lying down can be helpful if you are not feeling so confident with these strategies yet

◆ Set your timer for two minutes

◆ Without over-thinking it (remember there is no 'right' or 'wrong' with this), breathe in and out. When you breathe out pay attention to how long your exhalation is. Measure it by counting slowly in your mind: 1, 2, 3… (You're not trying to measure it in precise seconds – this is your own measurement)

◆ After several breaths (both an inhale and exhale counts as one breath), you should have a rough idea of the 'length' of your breath. Let's say it's 5. Now try to extend the exhalation for one more count so the length becomes 6, emptying your lungs of more air

◆ When you inhale, do so naturally, not taking in any more or less air than you would normally

◆ Continue counting your exhalations until the timer sounds

Review: How did you find this strategy? Because you were 'doing something' (counting) did you find your mind wandered less? Counting can help you to stay focused, but as you become more experienced you won't need to count, you'll simply be able to follow your breath. Whenever you have a spare two minutes practise until you can reach the timer without your mind wandering (although if it does wander, just gently bring it back to the task).

This strategy will break habitual responses to stress, anxiety and rumination. It's forcing your mind into the present, rather than mulling on old memories or panicking about what's coming in the future. By focusing on the breath you are anchoring yourself to the present so you can get some much-needed distance from your thoughts. These breathing exercises are a great foundation for upcoming formal practices.

Thoughts to take away

✓ Fight or flight, memories, senses and your upbringing all combine to form the stories your mind tells you in response to events

✓ Acknowledging what your mind is doing and why it's doing it will limit the power of stressful thoughts

✓ Use the breathing strategy to break habitual negative cycles of thoughts and memories and to lessen the effect of the fight or flight response

5

Deactivating Autopilot

Your inner autopilot function is brilliant – for certain things. When it's switched on for everything though, you end up just going through the motions. Here we teach you how to deactivate autopilot so you'll feel more awake, more present and can reclaim lost hours in your day.

Autopilot: the pros and cons

For much of our lives we live on autopilot. When you sit down to eat you don't talk yourself through every little thing you do: 'I'm going to cut the fish with my knife and fork, place the fish in my mouth with my fork, remove the fork, chew and then swallow the fish'. You just eat and hopefully enjoy the food. This is down to 'thought processing' – how our minds manage thoughts in an efficient way, siphoning off information it deems inconsequential, so you can multitask.

Autopilot is essential in life. Without it you wouldn't be able to function properly as there would be too much information clogging up your brain. If you had to think, step by step, through every tiny thing you did life would be painfully sloooow. Instead, autopilot turns certain things into habits, which, once learned, become instinctual. Things like: touch-typing, running, going to bed, driving, playing a piece you know well on an instrument, drinking or brushing your hair. These are all activities you can do while thinking about other things.

Autopilot allows you to undertake complex tasks with very little input from the conscious mind at all, freeing up space for the things that need more attention. This is brilliantly effective – but only when used properly. When you're busy, distracted or living in your head tasks can become automatic that shouldn't and life can start passing you by. For example, bashing out your work with minimum effort because you're thinking of your evening plans, or phoning your dad while watching the TV. Autopilot can also physically dominate your actions. How many times have you:

✦ Returned to your house to check you locked up because you can't remember whether you did or not?

✦ Realised you're going the wrong way on the bus or that you've driven past your turn-off?

✦ Wandered into a room, only to realise you have no idea what you went in there for?

Autopilot is designed for everyday routine tasks like brushing your teeth, walking or getting dressed. It's not meant to be used for things that need focus and concentration. When it's abused in this way, autopilot is the very definition of 'unmindful', making you feel as if you're floundering or disconnected from other people and events. By just going through the motions days pass in a blur ('How is it June already?').

⑤ A taste of mindfulness

In this strategy you'll eat a raisin mindfully. No, we're not kidding. Raisins are the kind of snack that you wolf down without thinking about it. You don't even taste them while you're throwing them into your mouth. Why? Because you're on autopilot; you normally eat them while you're doing something else. By trying to eat one mindfully you'll be breaking your autopilot habit and becoming present in the moment.

You'll need: a timer, a raisin, your notebook and a private space. Read the instructions through once and then go for it. Try not to stop and re-read unless you absolutely have to (consider recording the instructions and then listening as you go if you can't remember them). Spend at least 30 seconds on each instruction.

Set your timer for five minutes and get started:

1 **Hold:** Place the raisin in the palm of your hand or between your finger and thumb. Imagine you've just dropped in from Mars and have never seen an object like this before in your life.

2 **Touch:** Turn the raisin over between your fingers, exploring its texture. What does it feel like – rough, smooth, bumpy? Consider closing your eyes to enhance your sense of touch.

3 **See:** Really look at it. Observe where the light hits it – what patterns does the light make? Are there darker hollows? Are there folds and ridges in the skin? Is it bruised or scarred at all?

4 **Smell:** Hold the raisin beneath your nose and inhale deeply. Does it have

an aroma? Do you like the smell? Does your mouth water as you inhale?

5 **Move:** Slowly bring the raisin up to your lips, noticing how your hand and arm know instinctually how and where to position it. Gently place it in your mouth, without chewing, noticing how your lips and tongue move to receive it. Spend a few moments exploring how it feels.

6 **Taste:** Prepare to chew your raisin, paying attention to how your tongue moves it in position in order to bite through it. Then, very consciously, take one or two bites into it. How does it taste?

7 **Swallow:** When you feel ready to swallow the raisin, see if you detect the intention to swallow as it happens – did your tongue push it towards the back of your throat? Did you swallow it before you actually meant to?

8 **Digest:** Can you feel the raisin moving down your throat and into your stomach? Or do you imagine you might be able to feel it? Take note of how your mouth and body feel now the raisin has gone.

Review: Note down some answers to the questions below:

A What were your initial thoughts on reading through the instructions. For example: 'I don't like raisins'; 'This is stupid'; 'What's the point?'; 'Even though I'm alone I feel embarrassed'

B Have you ever paid attention to how a raisin looks and feels before?

C How did it smell and taste? How did it feel in your mouth? Did it taste different to normal – stronger or more intense?

D Did you think at any point, 'I'm not doing this right'? Chances are you did – our self-critical nature can turn up anywhere, even when we're eating raisins!

E Did your mind wander and if so, to what? Did the raisin bring up memories, for example of childhood lunchboxes or holiday snacks?

F When was the last time you paid so much attention to what you were eating?

We've asked you to write down your answers so that you really consider them rather than just skimming over them or dismissing them. By assessing what happened you might realise, for example, that while you thought, 'This is stupid' at first, the taste of the raisin was actually more intense than normal, thus proving the point of the exercise.

Everyone will have a different reaction to this strategy – some people will love it, some will hate it and some will feel completely indifferent to it. Some people might have thought it so bizarre they didn't even do it! (If you were one of these people, ask yourself if that's ever happened with anything else in your life and how often your mind stops you from doing things?) These reactions are totally normal, but hopefully after completing the exercise you can see the intention behind it: to transform a simple experience you'd normally do on autopilot into something completely different. Normally you'd have finished the entire packet of raisins in 20 seconds without even registering how they tasted. We rarely eat mindfully – working through lunch, eating on the go or caught up in conversation or watching the TV. While eating like that isn't bad, it could be so much better. If one little raisin tastes infinitely more intense when you've taken time over it, imagine how amazing that roast dinner would be if you savoured it a little more.

Obviously this isn't just about food; life generally can be experienced more fully and intensely. How often do you go about your life with such openness as you did in that strategy? It was a pure, unaffected moment of mindfulness, where you employed all your senses as if you were experiencing something for the very first time. Toddlers have this feeling of wonder every day, exploring the world anew, not caught up in worry or regret. While we don't advise regressing to your two-year-old self, channelling some of that curiosity into your own life will make everything more vivid, colourful and meaningful.

Changing your autopilot settings with 'informal' mindfulness

If you want to become more mindful you need to change your autopilot settings. They were fixed years ago and need updating. By altering the settings you'll gain a much greater understanding of your own life and enhance all of your experiences. You'll also become more aware of automatic thinking patterns you fall into so you can recognise negative cycles and avoid well-trodden destructive paths or mental ruts.

The bottom line is: if you're stuck in your head, it doesn't matter where you are or what you're doing as you're not present at all.

Being constantly on autopilot, going through the motions while your mind runs through a labyrinth of plans, worries and regrets is no way to live. What's the point of planning great stuff if you're never present when they happen? Here are some times when you might have noticed this:

+ Seeing your friends, but thinking about work
+ Spending a holiday panicking about someone breaking into your house
+ Feeling self-conscious about your outfit all day at a wedding

Being present means feeling more connected with the world and the people around you. We bet there are some events in your life that really stand out: the moment your name was called when you won an award; holding your baby for the first time; finding out you got the job you'd worked so hard to get. You remember these moments, but it's as if the rest of life is just filler – things to fill the gaps between these very fleeting memorable events. How awful that the majority of life should just be filler! Becoming more mindful of the simple things will make them more interesting and make the really great things incredible.

The raisin strategy was the first step in learning to become more mindful of simple experiences in your daily life. By starting to pay attention to the things you normally do on autopilot you'll notice you feel more awake, both physically and mentally, because you're not just plodding through the day, you're consciously participating in it.

Leaving your comfort zones

You can get into routines – both emotional and behavioural – that keep your life 'safe'. Emotionally you indulge in the same old thinking patterns and behaviourally do the same old things day after day, never deviating from what you know. When you're doing familiar things your autopilot is activated, leaving you susceptible to well-worn mental and emotional ruts, which is why we're going to advocate messing with your routine.

Ⓢ Messing with your routine

Plan something in your diary every day for the next week that breaks up your normal routine (actually schedule it in so you're less likely to skip it). Start small and build up to the bigger things. Here is a table with some examples to give you an idea of what we mean:

	Monday	Tuesday	Wednesday	Thursday	Friday	Saturday	Sunday
Routine break	Sit in a different chair when you watch TV (or at the dinner table)	Go to a different sandwich shop for lunch	Cycle to work rather than getting the train	Choose a different gym class	Suggest after-work drinks with colleagues	Chat someone up on a night out	Look for that new job you've wanted for ages

Review: How many of the new things you planned did you actually do? Did you skip any of them and return to your old routine? If so, why? Chances are you thought reverting to your old routine would be 'easier' – you know what you're getting so it's less stressful, but where's the fun in never taking risks or experiencing new things? By associating 'new' with 'stress' you're taking a back seat in life. Being put under pressure sometimes is a good thing and breaking up the routine means stepping out of autopilot. Your reflexes and body will kick into gear and you'll feel more alert, excited and interested – more alive.

Most of us are creatures of habit. There's a comfort and security that comes with knowing what will happen next. While reassuring, staying within your comfort zone can mean you're always just going through the motions, never living spontaneously or feeling brave enough to risk experiencing negative emotions. Our minds get excited by new things; it's how we remain interested in the world. By stepping outside your comfort zone and snapping out of autopilot you'll build up your tolerance to stress.

Technology black-outs

Have you ever left your phone at home and panicked? 'What if there's an emergency?', 'How will I speak to my friends?', 'How will I know which bar to go to?' You get home and rush to it like a long-lost friend to check what you missed… one solitary text message from your service provider.

Standing at the bus stop? Check your phone. At a boring dinner? Check your phone. Even if you're at a great dinner you'll probably still check your phone. Why? Because the pull of your online life can be hard to resist. Not checking your emails or social media accounts can make you feel anxious – just as checking them constantly can. Why haven't they emailed me back? Why wasn't I invited to that party? Why hasn't anyone 'liked' or retweeted my last post? However, while you're busy living your life online, your actual life is passing you by. Ninety-nine per cent of the messages you receive or send aren't urgent. By not allowing yourself to clock off you're perpetuating an expectation that you are (and should be) always available (which is nonsense), as well as focusing your mind on unimportant things.

ⓢ Tech strategy 1: Phone black-out times

We bet the first thing you did this morning when you woke up was check your phone. No? Well, then you're in the minority. It's amazing how many times we reach for it without even realising we're doing it. To combat this mindless subservience, give yourself phone black-out times.

✦ Schedule an hour each day for a week when you put your phone somewhere that isn't easily accessible, for example, in a different room, out of hand's reach (i.e. not your pocket) and don't check it

✦ Choose a time when you shouldn't be working or aren't expecting anything urgent, perhaps first thing in the morning or last thing at night

✦ If you find yourself freaking out at the thought of this then restrict the first black-out to 20 minutes, extending the black-out by ten minutes every day until you reach an hour

Review: How did it go? Did you cheat and check your phone sneakily? Don't worry, just try not to tomorrow. Were you surprised by how often you went to check your phone before realising it wasn't in its usual place?

Hopefully this strategy will convince you that the world won't end because you didn't post that hilarious status update or that snap of your new shoes. By relieving yourself from unnecessary distractions you'll be more focused on real life. We bet after a couple of days you'll be surprised by how gloriously free you feel not being beholden to your phone. Incorporate this strategy into your day-to-day life even when the week's over. For example, have phone-free meals and phone-free commutes.

ⓢ Tech strategy 2: Log out of all your online accounts

✦ If you think you might be a little addicted to your online life then log out of all your accounts each time you finish using them, e.g. emails, social media and shopping sites. You'll then have to consciously log in again when you next go to check.

Review: Did you find this strategy refreshing or annoying? Were you surprised by how often you went to check something without thinking about it? Did you always log in again or did you sometimes think, 'Actually, I don't need to'?

Access is often too easy. You're standing in a queue at a coffee shop, press twice on a touch screen and suddenly you're in social-media land without even thinking about it. By logging out you'll have to make the decision to log in. You'll become more conscious of the act and you'll probably be surprised by how often you go to those sites out of habit rather than need or desire.

Instead of logging in, look around you, take in the sights and sounds. Have a breather! Just be.

Deactivating your autopilot settings

The following is a selection of strategies to start resetting your autopilot system, making you aware of things you'd normally do without thinking. Remember to try all of them a couple of times – you might be surprised by which ones work for you. Don't rush them and don't multitask. Take your time and do everything slowly and deliberately.

The review for each strategy is the same: when you've finished ask yourself how it went, what you noticed, whether you had any doubts and whether those doubts were answered during the course of the strategy. Also, remember not to get upset if your mind wanders, just notice where it's wandered to and then gently bring it back to the task at hand. (We've also included a quick version of each strategy called one-minute mindfulness as a simple way to get started.)

Ⓢ Showering mindfully

When you take a shower, where are you? Yeah, okay – we know where your body is, but where's your mind? At work? Still in bed? For most people a shower is part of their wake-up routine, which means, more often than not, their minds are reeling with plans, worries and thoughts on the day ahead. There's usually at least one other person in the shower with them: their boss perhaps, a friend they're meeting later in the day, the driver who cut them up on the road yesterday.

This strategy is all about taking a shower mindfully, so you're fully present in the moment, rather than stuck in the past or battling the future.

✦ Step into the shower and notice how the water looks as it sprays down and pools at your feet. How does the water feel as it kneads your skin? What does your shampoo smell like? Is the room steaming up? Employ all your senses

It may help to say these things to yourself as a way of keeping your wandering thoughts focused on what you're doing:

✦ Breathe in
✦ I know I'm taking a shower
✦ Breathe out
✦ I can feel the hot water kneading my skin
✦ Breathe in
✦ I can taste the water
✦ Breathe out
✦ I can hear it falling all around me
✦ Breathe in
✦ I can see swirling patterns of steam rising from around my feet
✦ Breathe out
✦ I can smell the perfume of my shampoo

One-minute mindfulness: Pay attention when you turn the shower on, watching the water gain power and tune in to how it feels when it first hits your skin.

Ⓢ Eating mindfully

The raisin strategy (see page 77) got you thinking about eating mindfully, but we want to take this further as eating is one of the things we tend to do most frequently on autopilot. To combat this, try eating one meal a day mindfully. To start with this is best done alone (so you don't seem rude to your bemused dinner guests). Once you've practised and are more fluent in it you'll be able to do it with others – truly savour every mouthful – without having to concentrate so hard.

As you eat, ask yourself:

+ What does it look like?
+ How does it smell?
+ How does my body react in anticipation: is my stomach rumbling? Does my mouth water?
+ How does it feel in my mouth?
+ How does it taste when I bite into it?
+ What can I hear? Is it crunchy? Does it pop?
+ How does it feel when I swallow it?
+ How is my body reacting to the next mouthful: if it's not bothered then why am I eating it?!

One-minute mindfulness: Take two mindful bites at the start of every meal and snack.

Ⓢ Listening to music mindfully

Some music is meant to be background music – that tinny muzak you hear in lifts and restaurants springs to mind – but all too often we don't pay attention to what's coming through our headphones or speakers because we're too busy listening to our mind instead.

Next time you're listening to music make sure you actually hear it:

+ What instruments are playing or effects used?

+ Can you notice pitch changes?
+ Is there an effect used on the voice singing?
+ What are the lyrics?

One-minute mindfulness: Listen mindfully to the intro of each song.

S Listening to people mindfully

A simpler listening strategy, but possibly a more important one, is to start really listening to people when they're talking to you. When you're caught up in your own head often you either miss what they're saying or are simply waiting for your own opportunity to speak. Stop – this is rude and frustrating for the person you're with and means you won't remember details of the conversation later. You're behaving as if what's going on in your head is more important than what they're saying. If you're constantly forgetting what people have said ('Oh, you're going on holiday tomorrow?', 'Since when did you apply for a new job?'), you're simply not listening. Start paying attention and you'll be surprised by how much you learn and how much more interesting everyone suddenly seems!

One-minute mindfulness: Ask a relevant question during every conversation you have tomorrow.

S Hello world

This is a general, informal mindfulness strategy that you can do anytime, any place to become more aware of the world around you. The next time you're walking from A to B, instead of checking your phone or watching your feet, look around and employ all your senses:

+ What sounds can you hear? Cars, birds, people talking or laughing, horns blaring or planes humming?
+ What can you see? Are the buildings old, new, beautiful, ugly? Is there

graffiti? What are the people wearing? What colours are the leaves on the trees?

✦ What can you feel? Is the air cold or warm? Is it raining?
✦ What can you smell? Grass? Food? Flowers? Rubbish?

One-minute mindfulness: Pay attention to the feeling of the air on your skin for a minute while you're walking.

Other mindful activities you can try

Here is a list of simple things we normally do on autopilot that you can try to do more mindfully, to practise living in the moment. All you have to do is concentrate on the sensory stimuli at each stage – sight, sound, taste, smell, touch:

✦ Make and drink a mug of tea
✦ Do the washing up
✦ Brush your hair
✦ Take exercise
✦ Brush your teeth

A good tip is to set a reminder to go off at a certain time each day, to jog your memory to be more mindful. Then, whatever you're doing at that precise moment, you can try to do it more mindfully. So, if you're writing an email, really concentrate on it or if you're speaking to a friend, focus on what they're saying. Don't let your mind drift.

Ⓢ Your anti-autopilot log

Pick one of the mindful strategies in this chapter and try to do it every day for a week. Or vary the strategies each day. For example, brush your teeth mindfully on Monday or listen to music mindfully when you're travelling to work on Tuesday.

Use the table below to keep track of how you get on:

Day/date	Mindful activity	Comments
Monday	Hello world – focused on world around me rather than my phone during walk to work	I was surprised by how quickly the walk went compared with when I'm checking emails
Tuesday	Showered mindfully in the morning	I realised that my boss was always in the shower with me, which was pretty disconcerting. I felt better kicking her out
Wednesday	Listened to my favourite album	I noticed that some of the lyrics were actually very beautiful. It made me like the album even more

Review: Were you tempted to skip the mindful tasks you'd set yourself? Once you did them, did you feel a sense of achievement? Did your experience of these everyday events change?

Filling in this table should prove the difference deactivating autopilot can have on your life. Simple everyday tasks become more meaningful and you stop just going through the motions.

Thoughts to take away

✓ Breaking your autopilot patterns will reclaim the lost minutes (or hours) of your day

✓ If you're always stuck in your head it doesn't matter what you're doing, where you are or what you achieve – you're never present anyway

✓ If one raisin can taste so much better just by concentrating on it, imagine how amazing bigger, more important moments of mindfulness will feel

6

It's Written on Your Body

It's easy to ignore your body when it's trying to tell you it's run down, exhausted or stressed. Learn to reconnect with yourself physically and you'll have more choices in how to respond to events, thoughts and emotions.

The mind-body link

Think of a sexual fantasy. No really, please do – we'll wait. Now, focus on your body. Are your eyes dilating, heart racing, nerves tingling? It's the same as your mouth watering if you think about eating something truly delicious. Your mind and body are designed to work in tandem.

Your body is acutely sensitive to the tiniest flicker of emotion and thoughts galloping through your head: lips twitching when you're amused or fists clenching when you're furious. These non-verbal cues are how we read people, how we know, without words, whether they're happy, sad, angry, frustrated or nervous. Non-verbal cues are instinctual, involuntary and universal: everyone exhibits emotions through their physicality (unless they're experts in deception).

The mind-body link is bi-directional. For example, happiness can make you smile just as smiling can trigger feelings of happiness. In 1988 Professor of Psychology Dr Fritz Strack undertook an experiment to test this out. Researchers told able-bodied participants that they were studying adaptations in people who had lost the use of their hands (they weren't – this was a ruse). Half were asked to hold a pencil in their teeth (naturally activating the muscles used for smiling) and half were asked to hold the pencil between their lips (which doesn't activate smiling muscles). Those who were (unknowingly) 'smiling' rated cartoons as funnier than those who weren't, proving that grinning is one of the simplest, most effective ways to use your body to positively affect your mood – as is altering your posture. A study published in the *European Journal of Social Psychology* found that people who sat up straight instead of slouching were more confident about things they then wrote down. Participants also reported that standing straight with shoulders back and head held high increased feelings of social confidence. It makes sense – if you're hunched, with arms crossed, you're not going to feel like the life and soul of the party. Your body and mind share open channels of communication.

What your body is trying to tell you

Our bodies put up with a lot. The frenetic pace of our lives means we have a tendency to ignore or mistreat them, e.g. using caffeine to wake up and then mainlining it throughout the day, snacking on junk food for energy hits, using alcohol to calm down or sleep, taking drugs, ignoring aches and pains or not getting enough sleep. Maybe you don't like your body very much – it's let you down in some way by not looking or behaving the way you want. Or it's doing enough to get you through the day and that's all that matters right now. If you treat it as simply the vehicle that takes you from A to B you can become completely disconnected from how you feel physically, ignoring the warning messages it's sending you, leading to exhaustion or illness.

Your physical responses to situations are often the most obvious, so start paying attention. That constant nervous fluttering in your stomach isn't just annoying, it's flagging up your anxiety over something – what? You can use your body as a means to awareness, helping to identify moods and thoughts and to stop negative patterns establishing themselves.

The placebo effect

The 'placebo effect' is another example of the powerful link between mind and body. When given fake medicine (a 'placebo') tests have proven that people experience genuine physical (not just psychological) improvements. In 1996 scientists told a group of students that they would be testing a new painkiller called Trivaricaine. Not only did it have a suitably scientific-sounding name, but it even had that sour disinfectant smell associated with medicines. Trivaricaine was, in fact, just water, iodine and thyme oil – useless as a painkiller. It was painted on one index finger of each student, while the other was left untreated. Each index finger was then squeezed in a vice. All the students reported experiencing less pain in the treated finger.

⋯⋗

⋯∴ The students weren't stupid or playing along – they genuinely did experience less pain. Their minds expected there to be less pain and so informed their bodies this was so. Brain scans showed that expectation of pain relief actually caused the brain's pain-relief system to activate, 'numbing' the discomfort. The mind told the body what was happening and it responded accordingly.

⑤ Looking, and therefore feeling, more confident

There are two parts to this strategy:

1 During a single day take particular notice of your posture. Sit up straight, stand tall and make a conscious decision to keep your chin up. Also, be wary of defensive gestures such as crossing your arms or covering your mouth with your hand. If you notice yourself doing these things don't chastise yourself, just drop your shoulders, lift your chin, uncross your arms and straighten your back.

2 Smile more! Whenever you remember to, smile – when you're sitting at your desk, walking around or getting lunch. Don't plaster on a crazy Joker-style grin, just raise your lips a little and bring a half-smile to your face, even if smiling is the last thing you feel like doing.

Review:

A How did sitting up straight and standing tall make you feel emotionally and what did it make you think? Did being aware of your body in this way make you realise how often you slouch or put up defensive barriers? Did it improve your productivity because you felt more alert? Did you find that others responded to you differently?

B How did smiling more make you feel? What did you think? Did you notice others smiling in return? Smiles can be involuntary, for example, smiling when someone says 'Smile!' for a photo even if you're not in it.

Emotion-mapping

A team of scientists in Finland studied over 700 people to investigate where different emotions affect the body. The study, published in the *Proceedings of the National Academy of Sciences*, discovered that different emotional states were associated with culturally universal bodily sensations. They found that all emotions affected the face, i.e. your face reacts to every single mood across the emotional spectrum. Most basic emotions (happiness, sadness, anger or embarrassment) were felt strongly in the upper chest area, corresponding to changes in breathing and heart rate. So far, so expected. But then things got interesting. They found that both anger and happiness affected sensation in the arms, while decreased limb sensitivity was a defining feature of sadness. Sensations in the digestive system and around the throat were mainly found in those experiencing disgust. And, in contrast to all other emotions, happiness was associated with enhanced sensations all over the body. So basically, when you're happy your body thrums with life.

⑤ Tuning into your body

Take a moment to think about what happens to you physically when you feel the emotions listed below (we've included some examples that might help):

+ **Happy** (body feels 'lighter', stand up taller, chin raises, limbs feel relaxed, smile)
+ **Angry** (clench fists, grit teeth, furrow brow, curl lip, hunch shoulders, tense, feel hot)
+ **Sad** (slumped over, downturned mouth, bite lips, slack limbs, feel 'heavy')
+ **Anxious** (sweaty palms, wide-eyed, racing heart, rapid breathing, turn pale)

Review: When thinking about these emotions did you find yourself adopting the stances and physical positions they inspired, e.g. gritting your teeth or narrowing your eyes to emulate anger and sadness? If you did, did you then experience a flash of anger or sadness while in the position? Next time you're experiencing a specific emotion, check in with your body so you're aware of how you personally physically respond.

Most of the time you won't be aware that your emotions are written all over your body as you'll be too caught up in your mood or busy thinking about the event that's triggered the feeling. However, it's crucial to become more aware of it as your physicality directly affects your behaviour. For example, if you're nervous about the speech you have to give at a wedding your racing heart, sweaty palms and the blood pounding in your ears might prompt you to run away, hurdling over tables and chairs in your eagerness to escape – something you probably wouldn't have done had you been able to read the early-warning signs your body was providing.

Recognising how you respond physically to certain emotions will make you more aware of ensuing thought and behavioural patterns. The tension in your limbs, tightness in your chest and locked box in your stomach are your body's way of shouting 'WARNING – something bad could happen if you don't stop and pay attention!'

Ⓢ A mindful stroll

✦ Starting as soon as you finish reading this strategy, set your timer for three minutes and start to walk around, wherever you are. (If it's not convenient, for example, if you're on a packed bus, wait until you get off, but as soon as you're somewhere with room to stroll, please do.)

✦ Walk for walking's sake, without any destination in mind. If you actually have to get to work, take three minutes out just to walk around the block. Don't start walking to your office

The aim of this is to snap out of walking on autopilot. Focus on what your body is doing. How do your leg muscles feel? Do they ache/feel good? Are your shoes comfy? Concentrate on the movement of walking, moment-to-moment, aware of the sensations accompanying each step. Try not to analyse those sensations, that is, don't start wondering why your shoes pinch and whether you should get new ones and if so where from. Just register the physical feeling and move on.

Review: Did you enjoy your walk? Did it feel strange focusing so intently on something you'd normally do on autopilot? Did it feel good walking with no destination in mind?

We've all heard walking can help you chill out, but there's absolutely no point if you just stomp along, thinking about your anxiety. However, going for a mindful stroll really will calm down both your body and mind. Your body is always available as an anchor to the here and now and so serves as a perfect mindfulness tool. Getting in touch with your body in small ways (such as concentrating on walking or breathing) will help you live more mindfully day to day.

Example: Walking the walk

Mark hated his job and often found himself pounding away at the keys of his computer as though he wanted to crush them to pieces. He knew he was getting a reputation in the office as a firebrand; people made jokes about how they knew not to approach him if the vein on his forehead was pulsating.

One day the bound-up feeling in his chest was so severe he slammed his mug of coffee down on his desk and it smashed. A piece of china cut his hand and the hot coffee scalded his wrist. He swore loudly and ran to the bathroom.

···:

∴ A colleague followed him in and suggested that after he'd seen to his injuries he might go for a walk to calm down.

Mark walked around the block feeling furious, agitated and embarrassed. He took some deep breaths and remembered what his friend had told him about mindfulness. He tried to concentrate on the physical act of walking, focusing on how his legs moved and how his body felt rather than on his anxiety. He paid attention to the tightness in his chest and felt the tension ease slightly. When his angry thoughts returned, he consciously turned his attention back to his body.

After five minutes he felt calm enough to return to the office, where he apologised for his outburst. He could see the relief on people's faces when they saw his relaxed body language.

Mark's original mind map looked like this:

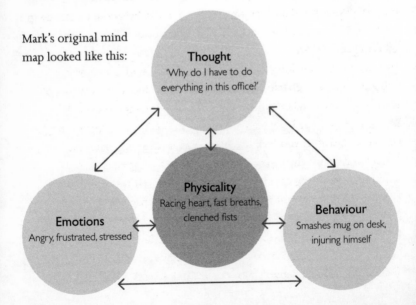

Thought
'Why do I have to do everything in this office?'

Physicality
Racing heart, fast breaths, clenched fists

Behaviour
Smashes mug on desk, injuring himself

Emotions
Angry, frustrated, stressed

Hopefully, the next time Mark experiences those physical symptoms (racing heart, tight chest, clenched fists) he'll recognise that he's at boiling point and take himself off for a (mindful) walk before he explodes, therefore breaking old negative cycles and creating new, more positive, ones.

Remember: simple things make the biggest differences.

A different perspective

Becoming aware of the sensations in your body will provide you with information you'd miss otherwise, giving you a new perspective from which to view your thoughts and emotions. Once you've realised what's happening to you physically, you're giving yourself a choice about how to proceed. Do you want to continue raging? If yes, fine – at least you're doing so by choice! If no, great – drop your shoulders, unclench your fists and go for a mindful walk or practise the body scan below. Calming down your body will have a knock-on effect on your mood, behaviour and thoughts.

Ⓢ The body scan

This strategy is quite long, but don't let that put you off as it's very important and very effective. It encourages you to focus on each part of your body separately, anchoring yourself in the present moment. Recognise how your body feels and accept it. Don't worry about trying to change or 'fix' what you feel; this is simply a strategy in awareness.

1 Go somewhere where you'll be undisturbed for approximately 20 minutes, removing any distractions. This strategy is best done lying down, but if you want to sit, see Chapter 3 (see page 47).

2 Take a few moments to get in touch with the movement of your breath. When you're ready, start focusing on the physical sensations in your body where it makes contact with the mat, bed or chair. On every exhale physically relax or 'let go', allowing yourself to sink a little deeper.

(You can close your eyes if you want to.)

3 Bring your attention to the physical sensations in your lower stomach, how it rises and falls as you breathe in and out. Take time, don't rush.

4 Swing your spotlight of focus down your left leg, into your left foot and onto your toes. Focus on each toe in turn, noticing the sense of contact between them – tingling, warmth or even that there's nothing to note.

5 When you inhale, imagine the breath entering your lungs and then passing into your abdomen, into the left leg, the left foot and out to the toes of your foot. Then, on the exhale, feel the breath come all the way back up – from the toes, to the leg, to the stomach, chest and out through the nose. Do this for several minutes, not worrying if you don't 'get it' straight away. If you're finding it difficult, just focus on the inhale – getting your breath to your toes.

6 Move your attention to the sole of your left foot. Concentrate on the instep, heel and any tingling. Notice the pressure where the foot touches the floor. Keep your attention on your breath in the background of your mind, while focusing on the foot in the foreground.

7 Expand your awareness to the rest of the foot – the ankle, top of the foot and into the bones and joints. Take a slightly deeper breath and direct it down into the whole left foot. As you exhale 'let go' of the foot and move your spotlight to the lower left leg: calf, shin, knee and so on.

8 Continue to bring this same curious awareness to the rest of the body in turn: the upper left leg, right toes, right foot, right leg, pelvic area, back, abdomen, chest, fingers, arms, shoulders, neck, head and face. As you leave each area, breathe into it on the inhale and let go of it on the exhale.

9 When you become aware of tension in a particular part of the body 'breathe in' to it – focus all your attention on the sensation you're feeling. Then 'let go' of the tension as you exhale.

10 If your mind wanders, register where it wandered off to and gently bring it back to the part of the body you were intending to focus on.

11 After you have 'scanned' your whole body, spend a few minutes taking in the body as a whole and on your breath entering/leaving it freely.

12 If you find yourself falling asleep, open your eyes and move to sit on a chair rather than lying down. If you're already sitting down, try to keep your eyes open until you finish the scan!

Review: What did you notice? What physical sensations did you experience? Did you feel any tension in your body? Did your mind wander? If so, where did it go? Did you manage to bring it back? Did you judge yourself or set yourself any rules?

It's quite normal, when doing the body scan for the first time, to be aware of negative, judgemental thoughts pinging into your head. Maybe you felt awkward, uncomfortable or ridiculous. Some people feel bored or even fall asleep. Some people can't feel sensations in parts of their body, making them think they're doing it wrong – they're not. That's natural. Everyone's different and everyone's body responds in different ways. Your mind might have added rules into the mix: 'don't fidget, don't move, don't think of anything else'. When thoughts badger you for attention use your breath to focus on your body. Try to view the thoughts as a curious, detached observer before bringing your attention back to the moment.

The scan shows you where and how the mind creates tension in your body and how, in turn, the body can create tension in the mind. As you meditate you'll start to see how the simple act of awareness can diffuse these tensions. Your body's trying to flag up that something's wrong and once it has your attention it'll calm down again.

Top tip: Try naming your thoughts as they enter your head: there are boredom thoughts/worry thoughts/planning thoughts/annoyed thoughts/embarrassed thoughts. By acknowledging them you're robbing them of their power.

Example: Helen's early-warning system

Helen noticed that as she became more aware of her body she became more aware of her emotions in everyday life. Using her body as an early-warning alarm system, she found she started recognising when anxiety was bubbling up. It normally started with a fluttery, nervous stomach accompanied by tense limbs and a racing heart.

Tuning in to these sensations gave her choices. She would leave the room, go for a walk, splash some water on her face or pay attention to her thoughts and work out what was making her feel that way. Sometimes she didn't catch her anxiety in time and still launched into full-blown fight or flight, but she was getting better at it and people started commenting on how composed she seemed.

Helen's mind map
looked like this:

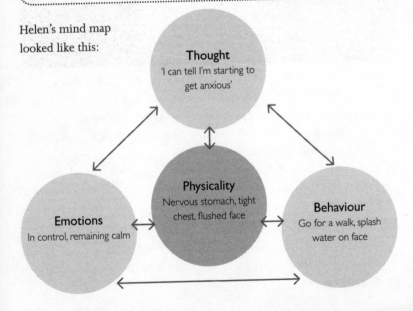

Thought
'I can tell I'm starting to get anxious'

Physicality
Nervous stomach, tight chest, flushed face

Emotions
In control, remaining calm

Behaviour
Go for a walk, splash water on face

By reconnecting to the different parts of your body – parts that you have most likely ignored for a while – you can relate differently to your thoughts, perceptions, emotions and impulses, giving yourself the freedom to choose what, if any, action needs to be taken.

Thoughts to take away

✓ Use your body as an emotion alarm system, warning you of potential inflammatory moods, so you can choose what happens next

✓ If you're feeling stressed or anxious, focusing on your body (by going for a mindful walk) will give you a break from all-consuming thoughts and emotions

✓ Practise the body scan to tune in to and reconnect with your body

7

The Path
of Most
Resistance

This chapter introduces you to your doing and being modes and teaches you how to avoid well-worn, destructive thinking paths that only make your stress, anxiety and low moods worse.

Doing versus being

Hopefully by now you agree that thinking is not all there is to conscious experience. You don't have to analyse, categorise, fix or solve every single little thing. You can also experience things through your senses, without words or thoughts clouding, confusing or complicating what's going on. You can just 'be', realising this is what mindfulness is all about. You need to start tuning into being mode rather than constantly being stuck in doing mode, which can lead you down destructive and negative paths.

Doing mode

Doing mode uses rational and critical thinking to problem-solve, comparing where you are to where you want to be and trying to find ways to bridge that gap. You need this mode – it's how you deal with practical tasks, e.g. building flat-pack furniture. It breaks the problem down into parts and presents different solutions to get you closer to your goal, reanalysing the steps as you go along to make sure it's working. It takes in both the past, hunting through memories that might present practical options, and also the future, looking for the best possible results.

For example, doing mode will kick in automatically if you've made plans to see a friend: 'Last time I took the train to Kate's (past), but we're driving this time, so I'll look up directions on a map (planning). There will be a football match on when we arrive (future) so we should avoid going past the stadium (planning)'.

Doing mode is automatic, initiated whenever you feel you need to plan/problem-solve. It's goal-focused: 'I need this; how do I get it?' It will no doubt have tried to interrupt you during some meditations, shouting, 'You need to do X, Y and Z – why on earth are you staring into space?'

This mode is fantastic for getting stuff done: everything from going to see your gran to designing a new computer game, flying to the moon or building a skyscraper is driven by this part of the mind.

Where doing mode falls short...

While doing mode is great for ticking things off your to-do list, it becomes problematic when it comes to emotions. It simply doesn't understand that emotions are not the same as practical problems and will try to find analytical means to 'fix' how you're feeling, which is impossible. Emotions are instinctual reactions to events and can't ever be wiped away or 'cured'. They are internal signals (to yourself) that something's going on and are your means of navigating experience. However, doing mode doesn't recognise this and will treat your mood as a practical conundrum, assessing where you are, where you want to be and evaluating the gap: 'I'm unhappy but I want to be happy. How do I get there?'

When presented with what it considers a 'problem', doing mode will try to 'solve' it. Take the 'I'm unhappy' example above: doing mode will go over all the possible reasons you're unhappy, asking questions that make you feel worse: 'Where did I go wrong? Why do I always make mistakes? Why hasn't this worked out? What events/people have made me feel this way? What will happen next?' Your mind is looking for reasons and evidence to back up how you feel and find ways of bridging the gap without realising that the questions it's asking are destructive. These angry, frustrated, self-blaming thoughts affect your body, emotions and behaviour, which feed off each other until you're a brooding mass of misery.

No animal (human or otherwise) likes feeling rubbish. We instinctually try to avoid negative emotions. This means we all too often rely on doing mode to try to think our way out of a sad, anxious, angry or stressed mood – but doing mode can't get rid of or 'fix' unwanted feelings, no matter how hard it tries.

Example: 'What's wrong with me?'

Nancy comes home after a reasonably successful day at work, kicks off her shoes, throws herself on the sofa and stares at the ceiling. She feels 'meh': uninspired, sluggish and grumpy. 'Why am I feeling like this?' she asks herself. 'What's wrong with me? Why aren't I happy? I wish I was feeling better.'

In asking herself these questions she activates doing mode – looking at the gap between where she is and where she wants to be. 'I should feel happier', she scolds herself. 'This is just like when I got my promotion and felt I didn't really care. I don't deserve my great job. Loads of people would kill for it and I'm not bothered. It isn't fair that I feel this way! I need to feel differently.'

Her heart rate picks up, her shoulders tense and she starts feeling sick.

Nancy's mind map looked like this:

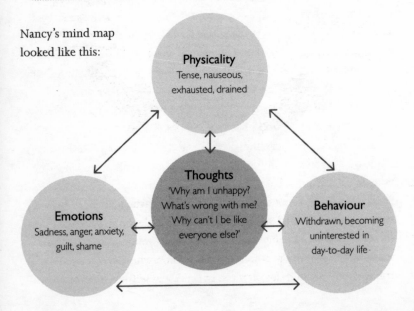

Physicality
Tense, nauseous, exhausted, drained

Thoughts
'Why am I unhappy? What's wrong with me? Why can't I be like everyone else?'

Behaviour
Withdrawn, becoming uninterested in day-to-day life

Emotions
Sadness, anger, anxiety, guilt, shame

By focusing on this gap (between where you are and where you want to be or feel you 'should' be) you get caught in a cycle of self-recrimination:

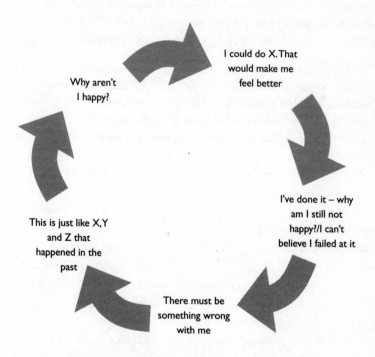

I could do X. That would make me feel better

I've done it – why am I still not happy?/I can't believe I failed at it

There must be something wrong with me

This is just like X, Y and Z that happened in the past

Why aren't I happy?

Doing mode is all about being goal-focused, but when you're constantly striving to achieve (and when you keep moving the boundaries for success) you end up being harsh and unkind to yourself. By constantly assessing the gap, you're constantly focusing on where you see yourself falling short, which heaps on more pressure and self-judgement.

Well-worn mind paths

Rumination and worry are the products of doing mode. While you may believe that brooding is helping you to think your way out of the problem, there's no evidence to back this up. You just tie yourself up in knots, circling round and round without producing a resolution (it's perhaps unsurprising that people who ruminate and worry are more predisposed to depression and anxiety disorders).

The more well-worn the path, the more instinctually you'll start travelling down it. Even small things can set you off, for example, hitting a 4pm lull and instead of thinking 'I'll perk up in a bit', thinking 'Why does this always happen to me? Why can't I stay motivated? What's wrong with me?' Before you know it you're at a point that bears no resemblance to where you started, pulled along by the thought/rumination/worry process. It's bad-mood autopilot. When you're stuck in a rut like this, you'll see bad things where there are none (interpreting neutral events as negative, e.g. 'He's talking about me') and feel worse. Common ways people try to combat feelings like these include drinking alcohol, taking drugs (medication or illegal), downing coffee or controlling food intake by over- or under-eating. All of which only add to the problem. The more you think, feel and behave in these ways, the more well-worn the path becomes, until you race down it without a second thought.

When you're in the midst of this vicious circle, it's near-enough impossible to step out and appreciate the good things – the little things that actually would make you feel happy if you noticed them: your partner bringing you a cup of tea, a beautiful sunny day or a compliment from a colleague. You're so caught up in striving to reach the next goal or wondering what's wrong with you that you never stop to appreciate your life as it is or what you've already achieved. You get dragged down in habitual patterns of thinking, behaving in ways you know are counter-productive, but can't stop.

Wait, though – there is some good news: mindfulness will make you aware of these well-worn paths and habitual negative spirals and offer you a new path to take instead. How? By recognising that trying to 'solve' a mood is useless. By acknowledging your emotions and stopping any attempt to 'fix' them, you won't tie yourself up in knots, but instead allow the mood to pass naturally ('I feel awful, but beating myself up about it won't help. I know I'll feel better soon'). Emotions are a natural consequence of whatever's going on in your life. By stopping your tendency to try to solve or get rid of them, they're much more likely to vanish. In short, you need to employ being mode instead.

Being mode: the antidote to doing mode

S 'Doing mode is not the only way of knowing'

Spend two minutes on each of these strategies:

1 Think about your feet and see where your mind takes you. Ask yourself some questions about them. For example, 'What do I think of my feet? Are they how I want them to be? How do they compare to other people's feet? What are they good for? What are they bad for?'

2 Now turn your focus to how your feet feel. What sensations are you experiencing? Are they hot or cold? What do they feel like inside your socks, in your shoes or resting on the floor? Scrunch up your toes and curl them. Hold them tight and focus on how this feels. Keep holding tight for as long as you can. How does it feel now? Release them and as you do so notice the sensations you experience.

Review: How did you find each part of the strategy? What did you notice when you were thinking about your feet? And, alternatively, what did you notice when you tuned into how your feet feel? What were the most striking differences between these two ways of knowing?

When you're analysing something – when you're in doing mode – you're likely to make associations that are good, bad or neutral. For example, cool water lapping over your toes on a hot day (good), a blister while running a marathon (bad) or realising you need to cut your nails (neutral). Your mind darts around, pulling you in all kinds of directions, including delving into the past or the future, such as thinking about the new flip-flops you need to buy for your holiday (future) because you broke your other pair last week (past). Meanwhile, being mode is all about sensations such as a tickle, pain, or an itch in your heel.

Being mode slows things down so that they feel less frantic. You don't need language, analysis and categorisation to be the intermediaries between you and the world – you can experience it directly through your senses. You don't need to think about your feet to tune into how they feel. You don't need to muse on chocolate to savour the taste. You don't need to analyse a flower to appreciate its scent. Your mind and body are linked rather than separate – your senses matter just as much as your thoughts.

In doing mode you experience things indirectly through thought and planning. In being mode you experience things directly as they happen. Being mode gives you the option of stopping a tidal wave of thoughts and emotions sweeping you along destructive paths, providing an opportunity to explore things experientially. You're not labelling, categorising or analysing. You're not trying to fix something or solve a problem. You're just being.

Being mode is what mindfulness is all about. It allows you to stay sensitive to your wider needs so you don't ignore your body; you don't ignore what's going on around you and give yourself choices. It's all about being present during happy, neutral and even distressing events – accepting them for what they are. This will make happy times happier and horrible times more manageable. By being open and letting go of your need to analyse and 'fix' everything, you'll gain a new perspective.

⑤ The sound of mindfulness

This strategy will take three minutes. Please set your timer and go somewhere where you won't be disturbed.

+ Sit down in the recommended way (see page 47) and either keep your eyes open, looking at something neutral, or close them
+ Now listen to the sounds around you without labelling them. We've been raised to use language to define our experience, analysing, categorising and 'solving' everything, but the point of this strategy is just to hear the sounds. Your mind will try to do it automatically: 'That's a bird', 'that's a phone', 'that's a car alarm – wait, what if it's my car alarm?' If it starts analysing or wandering off on tangents, just gently bring it back, without anger or judgement

Review: What did you notice? Did your mind wander off? If so, where did it go – into the future or the past? Did it make good, bad or neutral associations? Did you manage to hear any sounds without labelling them? Did you judge yourself or the exercise? How does this exercise change the more you practise it – what changes do you notice between the first time you do it and more recent times?

You can experience things, life around you, without always having to categorise them or solve them. When you analyse something, doing mode kicks in and tries to find practical links: 'That's a bird. You've heard that bird before', triggering emotions and memories. This is about learning to experience things in the moment without labels or categories and the ensuing baggage they bring with them.

Example: Jenny's housemate

Three months in and Jenny was regretting her decision to move in with her old school friend Becky, who was always out and never invited her along. Jenny felt lonely and often found her mind wandering into the past: 'This is the third time she's been out this week. I wish I hadn't moved in with her', and into the future: 'This is only going to get worse.'

Jenny was upset, angry and defensive and started snapping at Becky when she was in. She knew it was only making things worse, though, and started blaming herself for that too. When she felt like this she found it difficult to do anything but dwell on how bad things were. One day she practised the sound of mindfulness strategy. At first she found it difficult not to label every single sound she heard (for example, the clock ticking or the traffic outside) and her mind would soon jump to Becky, causing a familiar pang of angst. She practised, though, and over time found that she got better at simply hearing sounds without naming them and that gradually she became more aware of when and where her thoughts wandered.

Did the strategy make those evenings home alone more pleasant? No. Did it stop her making judgements, allow her to get out of her head for a bit and stop her snapping at Becky? Yes! Did it stop her self-recrimination cycle? Well, she was getting there. By getting out of her head she stopped adding to her distress by dredging up past and future times she'd felt terrible. Just being aware of the negative paths she was going down gave her perspective, making her feel calmer and more compassionate to both herself, Becky and the situation.

Doing mode versus being mode: the facts

The following table summarises the differences between doing and being modes. It's important to remember that sometimes you need doing mode, but only for practical matters, for everything else pick being mode every time.

Doing mode	Being mode
Autopilot	Conscious awareness and choice
Think/analyse	Directly experiencing
Dwell on past/worry about future	Being in the present
Avoid/escape/get rid of unpleasant feelings	Approach feelings non-judgementally
Need and want things to be different	Allow things to be as they are
View thoughts as real and true	View thoughts as mental events
Prioritise goals	Sensitivity to wider needs

Ⓢ Which mode are you in?

Set a reminder at either the same time or a different time each day (on your phone or in your diary) to check what mode you're in:

+ Are you in doing or being mode?
+ Are you thinking about OR experiencing what's happening now?
+ Are you in the best mode for what you're doing?

We want you to learn how to switch from one mode to another. For example, when you're deciding where to go for dinner you should be in doing mode, but when you arrive you should switch to being mode. Doing mode allows you to choose the best restaurant and get there, while being mode allows you to enjoy the evening. If you stayed in doing mode you'd spend the whole meal wondering how it's going, whether everyone's having a good time and what you should be doing to make the evening better, rather than savouring both the food and the company.

Learning to accept difficult emotions

We're all agreed that bad stuff happens to everyone; there's no avoiding it. This inevitably means that bad emotions happen to everyone too. You can't stop those either, but you can choose what happens next: either you continue in doing mode, getting sucked into negative thought quicksand, or you switch to being mode, recognise what's happening, step outside your chattering head, reflect and observe. Being aware of your thoughts gives you a choice – do I want to get sucked into them? The second option sounds better, right? Well, remember it, because it's often when you're at your most stressed that your mind sneers at mindfulness and tricks you into thinking that you don't have time for it. 'Mindfulness? Why bother with that? It's stupid.' DON'T LISTEN TO THESE THOUGHTS. They're trying to persuade you to charge down the same old negative paths.

Ⓢ Three-minute breathing space

This strategy will help you regain a compassionate mindset, dissolving negative thinking patterns before they grab you by the throat. It's a great way to stay focused when you feel under pressure, allowing you to pause, reflect and gain perspective. It concentrates the core elements of mindfulness into three steps of roughly one minute each. The three steps are:

1 **Becoming aware:** Switch off autopilot and recognise and acknowledge your experience in the moment
2 **Focusing attention:** Bring your attention to the breath and use your breath as a grounding focus
3 **Expanding attention:** Get a sense of the breath and the body as a whole

This strategy will be most effective if you can practise it twice a day – write it in your diary for next week. It's only three minutes long, so shouldn't be too hard to fit in.

Step 1 Becoming aware

Adopt our recommended meditation pose (see page 47) and close your eyes. Ask yourself, 'What is my experience right now?'

+ What thoughts are going through your mind? Acknowledge them and then let them go
+ What are you feeling emotionally? Turn towards the feeling. Acknowledge it without getting into it
+ What are you feeling physically? Concentrate on your body. Perhaps do a quick body scan to pick up any sensations of tightness or tension. Acknowledge them, but again, don't try to change them

Step 2 Focusing attention

Spotlight your attention on the physical sensation of your breath.

+ Concentrate on your abdomen as it expands when you inhale and contracts as you exhale
+ Follow the breath all the way in and out (perhaps counting it as you did in earlier strategies)
+ If the mind wanders gently escort it back to the breath

Step 3 Expanding attention

Expand your attention to include the entire body.

+ Imagine your whole body is breathing, picturing the breath travelling into every part
+ Zoom in on any sensations of discomfort, imagining the breath moving into and around the feeling and then 'letting go' of the tension as you exhale
+ Think of this as a way of exploring the sensations without trying to change them. If they stop pulling for your attention, just sit, aware of your whole body moment by moment

This strategy can be illustrated as an hourglass:

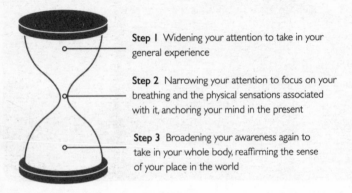

Step 1 Widening your attention to take in your general experience

Step 2 Narrowing your attention to focus on your breathing and the physical sensations associated with it, anchoring your mind in the present

Step 3 Broadening your awareness again to take in your whole body, reaffirming the sense of your place in the world

Review: What thoughts, sensations or urges did you notice? Reconnecting with your breath helps you to sidestep judgements, criticisms and categorisations that may arise from a belief that you're doing the strategy 'wrong', proving how easy it is to get impatient and frustrated with yourself. This strategy is perfect for when you notice your mind wandering down negative paths or when you realise your body is reflecting your feelings of emotional angst. It will remind you to stop obsessing over desired outcomes or wanting things to be a certain way, teaching you to be more patient and compassionate with yourself. This will free you from the destructive pull of stress, unhappiness and anxiety. Instead, you can just 'be'.

Thoughts to take away

✓ Both doing mode and being mode have their place. Just make sure you're in the right mode at the right time

✓ Mindfulness will help you avoid well-worn negative thinking paths that only exacerbate feelings of stress, anxiety and low mood

✓ Emotions can't be fixed or cured. They're your way of navigating experience. Even the bad ones have a purpose!

8

Let it Be

Your mood can't be fixed or solved. This chapter looks at how accepting emotions, even the awful ones, is the only way to ensure they'll pass without inflicting lasting damage.

Feeling-tones

When something happens, depending on what it is, you'll experience emotions that will induce one of three different overall 'feeling-tones':

1 **Pleasant/good feelings:** ones you'd like to hold onto
2 **Neutral feelings:** ones that don't affect you positively or negatively
3 **Unpleasant/bad feelings:** ones you try to push away or avoid

Feeling-tones are experiences of agreeableness or disagreeableness, pleasantness or unpleasantness that accompany certain emotions. For example, if you win the lottery you'll feel elated, surprised and excited, inducing great feeling-tones, an all-over sense of 'Wahoo!' If your cat dies, you feel grief and sadness, evoking a general sense of unpleasantness.

On the whole, we want to make pleasant feeling-tones last, so we try to hold onto them. With neutral feeling-tones we usually zone out and disconnect from our experience. However, with negative feeling-tones we tend to try to get rid of them or try to prevent them happening again.

Feeling-tones are subtle – you may not even be aware of them as they come and go, yet they have a massive influence over what comes next, triggering certain thoughts and behaviours. We'd all love to feel brilliant all the time, but it's just not realistic. Bad things happen and you respond to them emotionally. You're going to feel awful, annoyed, frustrated, humiliated and anxious at times; it would be unnatural if you didn't. Whatever negative emotion you experience will generate unfavourable feeling-tones – a general sense of 'eugh'. As it's human nature to hate disagreeable things, it's natural to try to battle negative feeling-tones by trying one (or all) of the following tactics:

1 Trying to get rid of the emotions
2 Trying to ignore/avoid them
3 Dwelling on them or obsessing over them
4 Trying to stop them happening again

This table shows some common methods associated with these tactics:

Negative feeling-tones inspire you to...	What this involves	The result
1 Try to get rid of them	✦ Activate doing mode to try to 'fix' your mood (which is impossible) ✦ Ask lots of why questions: 'why do I feel like this?' ✦ Live only for the future and set unrealistic/unhelpful/pointless goals: 'If I do X,Y and Z I'll feel better' ✦ Dwell and worry: 'Why can't I just get over it/be happy?'	Self-recrimination and feelings of failure when your mood isn't 'sorted out'. You can't just get rid of unpleasant emotions or think your way out of them. By focusing on this impossible task and/or by dwelling on the past you miss the good day-to-day things that would naturally lift your mood
2 Ignore/avoid them	✦ Distract yourself ✦ Deny painful feelings: 'I'm feeling great, thanks!' ✦ Mask them with alcohol, drugs or by becoming a workaholic	By distracting yourself, denying the feelings or masking them with alcohol, drugs or work you're just kidding yourself. The feelings will loom over you like your own personal rain cloud. Avoidance might work in the short-term, but you can't keep the feelings at bay indefinitely
3 Obsess over them	✦ Wallow in the feeling ✦ Pick over and over the event that inspired it ✦ Relish feeling low because you deserve to feel bad ✦ Ruminate on past experiences that triggered the same feelings	Whatever emotion originally inspired the feeling-tone (anger, humiliation, envy, anxiety, sadness) you end up piling on more in the form of guilt, shame, anger or even more sadness by ruminating, worrying and comparing yourself to others (the second arrow, see pages 142–3). You're so wrapped up in your mood you're missing life
4 Try to stop them happening again	✦ Avoid situations or events that might inspire the same feelings by isolating yourself or sticking to rigid routines	You create a comfort zone and stay within it, limiting your experiences. It's impossible to stop unpleasant feelings altogether and trying to do so only ensures bad stuff hits you twice as hard the next time around

Mindfulness is about letting these so-called 'bad' emotions be; learning to leave them alone. 'What?' we hear you cry. 'You want us to feel bad?' Yes. Because feelings pass. It's that simple. No feeling will last forever, no matter how hideous it is. Yet by employing any of the tactics listed on the previous page you'll be making it hang around longer than it would if you just waited for it to pass naturally.

Your 'I don't want to feel like this' response is totally understandable, but your emotions are there for a reason. They are our way, as humans, to process what's happening to us. Avoidance, preoccupation, worry and rumination stop them from being able to do their job. That old saying, 'What doesn't kill you makes you stronger' is true. Difficult emotions will make you a stronger person if you let them take their course. You can't learn, grow or move on if you're constantly running away from emotions you dislike. The only way they'll go away is if you face them head-on.

Ⓢ Turning towards sadness

This strategy is adapted from *Teaching Clients to Use Mindfulness Skills*, Dunkley & Stanton.

+ Set your timer for two minutes, grab a notebook and sit somewhere quiet where you will be undisturbed

+ Now, turn your mind to sadness. Think about how you feel when you're sad and what those feelings prompt you to do or think about doing.

+ Start each sentence, 'I'm aware that when I'm sad…' then focus wholly on the feeling, trying to conjure it up. For example, 'I'm aware that when I'm sad I sometimes feel like crying. I'm aware that when I'm sad I often eat lots of biscuits. I'm aware that when I'm sad my chest feels tight. I'm aware that when I'm sad I turn to my friends for support/ hide myself away'

You can say each point out loud or write them down.

Review: How did you find this strategy? Did you skip it altogether? (Be honest.)

We asked you to turn your mind to something you would normally actively try to turn away from. Often people are worried about where this strategy might lead them, however most people who complete it report that it wasn't actually as bad as they feared it might be. The point is to realise that you can tune into sadness…and tune out again. You can dangle a foot over the edge of the cliff without falling off it. This should reassure you that there are degrees of unhappiness, a continuum that you can move up and down, so that when something bad does happen you won't automatically fall into a hideous, dark abyss. By being able to think about sadness you're on the road to being able to tolerate it. It doesn't have to consume you and acknowledging that means it won't. Facing your fears can be hugely liberating as you'll know what you're dealing with.

Learning to let things be

The strategies throughout the book so far have been leading to this point – putting everything you've learned into practice so you can accept emotions and thoughts as transient events that don't define you, but which you can use as a guide to being more present (more on thoughts in the next chapters).

It's possible to suspend your normal ways of relating to negative experiences so that you get a better and fairer perspective rather than letting stress or worry suffocate you. By just letting things be, you'll become calmer, kinder to yourself and more accepting. This isn't the same as being resigned, sighing and washing your hands of anything tough or challenging; it's about learning that you don't have to be constantly fighting to feel a certain way. By being mindful, stress becomes less stressful and happiness, joy and pleasure become more happy, joyous and pleasurable. It's a win-win situation.

Example: Ed's exam

Ed discovered that he'd failed an important exam. As he read the 'I'm sorry to report…' line his stomach dropped and he felt tears prickling at the back of his eyes. The thoughts 'I must be really stupid' and 'I've let everyone down' pinged into his mind.

The un-mindful response: Ed's thoughts spiralled until he was ruminating on past 'failures' and times he'd let his parents/colleagues/friends down. Ashamed, he didn't tell anyone he'd failed, trying to buy himself some time and avoid the subject, but they found out through other people and were upset he hadn't told them himself. This made him feel guilty on top of embarrassed, upset and angry. He could re-apply to take the exam, but he decided not to – he didn't want to feel this way again. He'd just stick to what he knew he was good at.

The mindful response: Ed recognised that his mind was scraping around for evidence to back up the 'I'm a failure' story. He also recognised his body was reacting to these thoughts by feeling tense, anxious and sick. He took some deep breaths, focusing on his body and breath as an anchor and managed to step back from his thoughts and feelings. 'Okay, I feel bad,' he acknowledged, 'and failing the exam will cause me some problems, but they're nothing I can't handle. At least I was brave enough to take it in the first place.'

Being mindful doesn't mean you stop planning for the future or trying to improve your life. It just gives you the tools to make educated plans and decisions rather than letting your emotions and thoughts (which aren't always helpful) decide for you.

Cultivating an attitude of acceptance, calmness and compassion

By turning towards unpleasant thoughts and feelings, breaking negative patterns and learning how to leave your comfort zones you'll become more mindful. As you already know, your emotions exhibit themselves physically, so turning towards your body as well as your thoughts is a key part of facing tough emotions head-on. By using your body as an early-warning distress system you'll avoid exacerbating anxiety, worry and sadness. Your body feels things for a reason. By incorporating these steps into your life you'll reverse your habitual rejection of anything difficult or unpleasant and instead start cultivating an attitude of acceptance and calmness.

Ⓢ Rejecting rejection

✦ Sit for a few minutes focusing on the sensations of breathing, before widening your awareness to take in the body as a whole

✦ When you're feeling totally present, bring to mind a current difficulty affecting your life. It doesn't have to be very important or critical, just something that's been clogging up your thoughts: maybe a misunderstanding or argument, a worry or situation in which you feel regretful, angry or guilty. If nothing comes to mind, choose something from the past

✦ Once you have the event or thought in your mind, tune into any physical sensations in the body. See if you are able to note and investigate inwardly those physical feelings, directing your attention to the region of the body where the sensations are strongest. Breathe into that part of the body on the in-breath and breathe out from that region on the out-breath, exploring the sensations, watching their intensity shift up and down from one moment to the next

✦ Once your attention has settled on the bodily sensations and they are vividly present in your awareness, unpleasant as they may be, try deepening the attitude of acceptance and openness to whatever sensations you are experiencing by saying to yourself, 'It's okay. Whatever it is, it's already here. Let me open to it,' then just stay with the awareness of these physical sensations and your relationship to them, breathing with them, accepting them, letting them be. It may be helpful to repeat, 'It's here right now. Whatever it is, it's already here. Let me open to it'

✦ Remember that by saying, 'It's already here' or 'It's OK' you're not judging the original situation or saying that everything's fine, but simply helping your awareness, right now, to remain open to the sensations in the body

✦ When you notice the bodily sensations are no longer pulling your attention to the same degree, return 100 per cent to the breath, making it the primary object of attention. If in the next few minutes no powerful bodily sensations arise, feel free to try this exercise with any sensations at all, even if they have no particular emotional charge

Review: What did you notice? Where did you experience emotionally charged bodily sensations the strongest? Becoming aware of where you personally experience physical unpleasantness will make you more receptive to it when it happens again so you know what to look out for.

Ed tried this strategy and noticed that it was difficult not to get drawn into the 'bad' feelings. His automatic reaction was to try and answer back to the negative thoughts. However, with time, he was able to simply link up how he was feeling and thinking, giving himself space to work through it. He found it helpful when strong emotions came up to name them, for example, 'The emotion of sadness is here', rather than 'I feel like I'm a failure', or 'The emotion of anger is here' rather than 'I can't believe I failed the exam'. He pictured his emotions as weather fronts: the stormy weather comes and goes, just as the bright, sunny weather does. Recognising these feeling-tones also made him notice where emotions affected him physically. His anxiety and shame were held as a tightness in his chest. Just realising this released some of the tension.

The point of meditation is to 'allow' these feelings and thoughts to come and go without getting into them. That means good feelings too. You don't want to hold onto anything either good or bad; you just want to 'be'. When the mind draws us to more pleasant feelings during the meditations, it can be tempting to stay there and enjoy the way it feels. When we make associations they can pull us in and take us away from the starting point; we can get completely caught up in them. Although it might seem that the good judgements, evaluations and associations are harmless, the aim is not to get hooked into either good or bad as both take you away from the moment. If you judge some things as good/better/right, then by definition there must be bad/worse/wrong. Mindfulness isn't about judging, fixing or wanting things to be other than they are. Whether we are pulled to good associations or unpleasant ones, the skill is still the same, to practise returning your mind to the present. This way even though it can be hard to leave a pleasant association, you're developing the skill so you can use it on a painful association.

Let go of trying to make things different. Allowing experience means simply allowing space for whatever is going on, rather than trying to create some other state.

Example: Singing in the rain

Sarah was cowering in a bus shelter after a sudden downpour of rain caught her unawares. She didn't have an umbrella and was wearing open-toed sandals – her feet were soaked within seconds. Ten minutes later and the rain hadn't eased off at all. If anything, it had got heavier. Sarah knew she couldn't avoid it forever – she'd have to face it eventually.

Her options:

A Run through it, cursing it as it drenches her, thinking, 'Why does this always happen to me?' or 'This is so typical! I'm going to have to wash all my clothes when I get home.' Her limbs tense up and she clenches her fists as she splashes along.

B Realise that getting angry or annoyed will only add to her discomfort. Noticing her physical tension, she takes deep breaths, focusing on her inhales and exhales. 'I'm having "this is so unfair" thoughts,' she thinks, 'they'll only get worse if I indulge them'. Instead she concentrates on the rain and how it looks kind of beautiful. Knowing she's going to get drenched whatever she does, she thinks, 'What the hell?' and strolls into it.

By choosing Option B Sarah changes her entire relationship to the rain, a very obvious but effective metaphor for emotions: you can run from them, avoid them, berate them, feel despondent about them or you can face them and let them be.

Here is Sarah's Option B mind map:

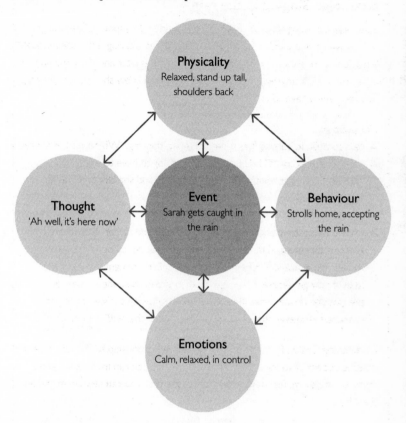

Physicality
Relaxed, stand up tall, shoulders back

Thought
'Ah well, it's here now'

Event
Sarah gets caught in the rain

Behaviour
Strolls home, accepting the rain

Emotions
Calm, relaxed, in control

Important things to remember

✦ Meditation doesn't 'work'. You can't do it right or wrong. Don't judge yourself or punish yourself if thoughts get in the way and your mind wanders. That's natural. Being mindful is about recognising when that happens and bringing your mind gently back to the present.

✦ Naming your emotions can help you to get distance from them just as naming your thoughts can (as discussed in Chapter 10, see pages 163–5): 'Here's the emotion of anxiety'/'Here's the emotion of sadness'.

✦ Take notice if your mind is repeatedly drawn to a particular place, to particular thoughts, feelings or physical sensations. Don't try to change this, reject it or fix it. Just accept it and turn towards it. Holding unpleasantness in awareness sends a strong message: 'I can face this and work with it. I'm not running away.'

✦ Mindfulness is about seeing things as they really are, rather than how you would like them to be.

✦ Let go of trying to make things different. Instead become aware of what 'is'. It will free you from getting pulled this way and that. Instead you can just be fully present in the moment.

Letting your emotions simply exist as they are, stepping back from them and not judging them stops what Thích Nhất Hạnh describes as 'the second arrow'. We go into this in more detail in Chapter 9a (see pages 142–3), but basically it describes the effect of thinking negatively on your emotions: if you get shot by an arrow it hurts (something bad happens to you), but if you get shot in the same place a second time it hurts much worse (by thinking over and over the event). You shoot yourself again with your reaction and pile guilt, shame, worry and angst into the mix. Learning to accept your emotions and let them run their course shifts your attention to the here and now and makes you realise that sadness, anxiety, despondency and stress can and will pass. Nothing is fixed forever. You can make changes – educated, mindful changes, so you feel more in control, more present and more alive!

Thoughts to take away

✓ You can't avoid, fix or stop emotions. By trying, you're just exacerbating and prolonging distress

✓ Use your body as a guide to register your mood. That's what it's there for – it's trying to tell you something, so listen to it

✓ Learn to let your emotions be. They don't have to dictate your life. By being aware of them in the moment you'll be truly present in the here and now and life won't pass you by

9a

Telling Tales

Your mind tells stories to try to make sense of events and feelings. The trouble is that often they're absurd, based on thoughts such as, 'I can't do this' or 'This is a disaster'. This chapter teaches you how to recognise and challenge such stories in order to get a fairer perspective.

Thoughts aren't facts

Imagine this: you're strolling down the street, minding your own business, when you see your friend Jake. You wave and call his name. Jake looks directly at you…then turns away. He doesn't wave or acknowledge you; he just carries on walking.

What just happened? The following table lists some common automatic thoughts triggered by this event and the subsequent emotions.

Event	Thoughts	Emotions
Someone you know doesn't respond to your greeting	'He ignored me!'	Upset, embarrassed, angry
	'I must have done something to upset him'	Anxious, nervous
	'I can't believe he didn't wave. That's so rude!'	Angry
	'Not surprising – no one likes me'	Isolated, lonely, despairing
	'Maybe he was in a hurry to get somewhere. I hope he's OK'	Concerned, calm
	'I don't think he was wearing his glasses; he must not have seen me'	Neutral, calm

By believing the thought that Jake blanked you, you might ignore him the next time you see him, causing a totally unnecessary chain of events. Whereas, if you were feeling more positive, neutral and, let's be honest, realistic about the situation you could say, 'Hey, I saw you the other day – did you see me?' and find out what actually happened without jumping to conclusions.

We've illustrated one of the interpretations concerning the encounter with Jake in a mind map:

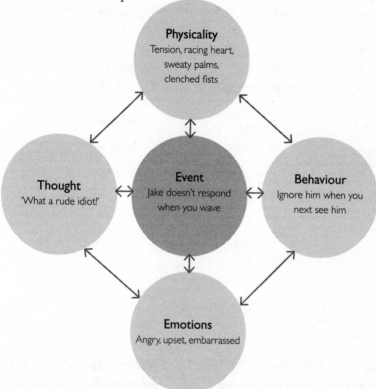

Physicality
Tension, racing heart, sweaty palms, clenched fists

Thought
'What a rude idiot!'

Event
Jake doesn't respond when you wave

Behaviour
Ignore him when you next see him

Emotions
Angry, upset, embarrassed

Here's another example. Imagine you've had a really terrible day: one of those days that makes you despair of ever getting out of bed again. On your way to work you walked through a filthy puddle in your new shoes before missing your bus. Then, when you finally arrived your tricky boss pulled you into a meeting room (a glass meeting room, so everyone could watch) and told you off for something that was all her fault. While your

Event	Thought	Emotions
Boss tells you off for something that's not your fault	'Not surprising; she hates me'	Resigned, low, despairing
	'This is so unfair'	Angry, frustrated
	'This is just typical! This kind of stuff always happens to me'	Annoyed, resigned
	'Ha! Everyone will know this isn't my fault. It's actually quite funny'	Calm, neutral
	'Maybe she's just having a bad day'	Neutral, calm

Here's what one of those interpretations looks like in a mind map:

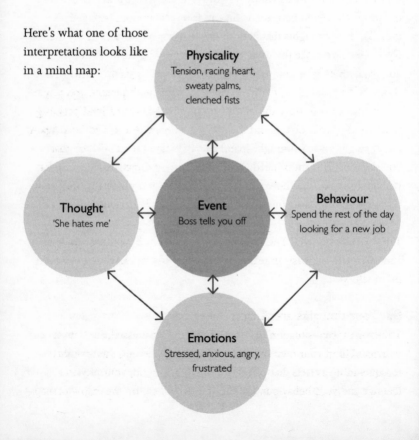

boss was shouting, you looked down and realised she was wearing the same shoes as you, except hers weren't wet and ruined.

What are your thoughts? What just happened?

It's scary how often we accept ridiculous thoughts as fundamental facts: 'My boss hates me' and 'This kind of thing always happens to me'. The mind is constantly telling us stories as it tries to make sense of what's going on, but it's often just guessing, filling in the gaps with opinions and hypotheses. Depending on our mood and the situation, the information it provides can throw us wildly off course as we accept it as true without question. When you have a tendency to feel low/anxious/stressed it's these kinds of thoughts that not only make you feel worse, but that have the potential to make the situation worse. Using the previous example, if you're an angry type you might snap at your boss or stamp on her pristine shoes. Not a good idea. If you're a bottle-it-up kind of person, you might storm back to your desk and pen a furious email to your friend detailing what an idiot your boss is and then accidentally send it to said boss. Again, not at all good. Or you might spend all day looking for a new job that you don't really want or need. Your thoughts will directly influence what you choose to do and how you feel emotionally and physically, so if your thoughts are negative your mood, physicality and behaviour will be too.

THOUGHTS ARE NOT FACTS. They don't represent how things really are and often have no basis in reality. You need to be wary of the stories your mind tells you.

S 'Your thoughts aren't facts' mind map

Think of a recent situation that caused you to feel stressed, anxious or worried. Fill in your own mind map detailing the event, the thoughts masquerading as facts that passed through your mind, your physical feelings and your behaviour. You can start anywhere on the map – perhaps you remember your body feeling tense (physicality) or you remember kicking a wall (behaviour) – and use that as your starting point.

Review: Were the thoughts you had about the event indisputable facts? Would they stand up to cross-examination? Can you see how your immediate thoughts triggered an unhelpful sequence of events?

NATs (negative automatic thoughts)

The thoughts we've been discussing are called NATs – negative automatic thoughts. They're nasty pieces of work that are determined to trip you up and make you feel terrible. They're lightning-quick, flashing through your mind before you're even aware of them, so you rarely question them, but just accept them as fundamental truths. When you're stressed/anxious/low your mind becomes biased to reflect how you feel, distorting information to fit your fears, triggering NATs. Your fight or flight reflex also gets involved, hunting out 'threats' and finding them wherever it can.

NATs affect your ideas and beliefs, how you speak to yourself and how you behave. If you allow them free rein in your head they'll make everything seem darker, gloomier and more insurmountable.

✦ NATs are the thoughts that whizz into your head without you even being aware of them. Things like: 'She's much more successful than me', 'I really messed that up', 'He's angry with me', 'I'm such a fraud'

✦ They are pessimistic appraisals and interpretations of things going on around you that you accept as facts

✦ NATs are unreasonable and unrealistic, but will often be based upon deep fears and insecurities so will seem reasonable to you no matter how ludicrous. For example, thinking 'Jake ignored me!' even though he has absolutely no reason to ignore you. Your mind will then try to find reasons why he might ignore you – and it will, because story-telling and evidence-gathering is what it's good at (see opposite)

✦ NATs are contagious. One can spiral into three, four or five. For example, 'He ignored me!' → 'I must have done something wrong' → 'I always do things wrong' → 'I'm useless'. All this because Jake forgot his glasses! Like Chinese whispers, before you know it you're feeling sad/worried about something that has nothing to do with the original event

✦ NATs make you feel terrible and stop you enjoying your life

Evidence-gathering

Why do you believe NATs? Because your mind gathers evidence to back them up and then shapes a story around them, like this:

Event → NAT → Evidence-gathering to support NAT → Your mind's story

Your mind puts together all the information it's gathered and then weaves intricate tales that fit your current mindset so you'll find them believable. It does this by tapping into your memories or fears of the future and presenting them as evidence to back up your mood and NATs. For example, 'Struggling at work? That's because you're rubbish at your job! Remember when you messed up that last project?'

This evidence-gathering and story-telling means the same event can have completely different meanings for different people. For example, while Natasha is really looking forward to the office Christmas party, her colleague, Jonny, is dreading it. He can't think of anything worse than enduring an evening of 'compulsory fun' where he knows (because his story-telling mind has informed him so) that he'll make a fool of himself, just like he did last year. This way of thinking will affect his mood and behaviour and he'll probably end up having a bad time, but not because of any external factors, but because he'll act like a right Grinch all evening.

Timing can play a big role too – the same event can have different meanings for the same person, depending on when it happens. For example, reading a terrible work email first thing on a Monday morning or last thing on a Friday evening. If you feel stressed your mind will gather evidence and shape a story around how, because it's Friday, your whole weekend is now ruined. Whereas if it's on Monday morning you might think, 'At least I've got a whole week to sort it out'.

Building a case against NATs and awful stories

Often our interpretations are based on familiar patterns and ways of thinking. The more you think a certain way, the more evidence you can find to back it up (such as 'Nothing ever goes right for me'). And any information that contradicts this version of events is ignored or dismissed (i.e. situations where things that have gone well 'don't count').

The tales your mind tells you should be treated with suspicion because they're being formed in a very biased, stressed-out place. Becoming more aware of them will give you opportunities to challenge them. 'Is it likely Jake ignored me? What reason would he have for doing so?' Even if they are true – even if Jake did ignore you – accepting the NATs without any perspective won't help. Suddenly he's a rude prat and you've vowed never to speak to him again. In reality he forgot your birthday and panicked when he saw you. Or he didn't know how to tell you he got that job you both went for. It's integral to be able to step back from NATs such as, 'He's so rude! He always does this!' and recognise them as opinions, not facts – before fight or flight kicks in and your logical mind does a runner.

The second arrow

As mentioned in the previous chapter 'the second arrow' describes the repercussions on your mood, body and behaviour of thinking negatively. If something terrible happens it hurts (the first arrow), but by indulging NATs you're shooting yourself twice, piling on more pain and aggravating the original wound.

Example: A baleful break-up

Simone's boyfriend Peter broke up with her while they were out house-hunting. Not only did he not want to buy a house, he wanted to end their five-year relationship completely. He'd actually decided to use his share of the deposit to go travelling and 'find himself'. Simone spent three days crying, thinking, 'How hideous must I be if he's leaving the country to get away from me? How could I have got this so wrong? What have I done?'

She called and called him, leaving weepy voicemails, until on the third day a friend answered and told her that if she didn't stop calling, Peter would have to block her number. The friend's pitying tone made her feel even worse.

In Simone's case (see box above), the first arrow is her relationship break-up – this hurts her deeply. The second arrow is her self-recrimination, worry and rumination, which aggravates the first pain, making it even deeper and more severe.

The first arrow Simone can't do anything about – it was Peter's decision and it's final. However, she can control the second arrow. She doesn't have to think those terrible things about herself. Yes, she will grieve for her ended relationship and feel sad, but that's all part of the first arrow. It's the self-recrimination, worry and rumination that will make the natural sadness much worse.

Shooting yourself with a second arrow is completely unnecessary and doesn't help anyone; it actually only makes things worse for you and everyone around you.

By becoming aware of NATs, second arrows and unhelpful behaviours you can make changes to ensure you're more in control, calmer and have the right tools to make the best decisions. You can start trying to use those thoughts as an early-warning alarm system: 'I'm going down this path again'. You can start to challenge them or just acknowledge them and move on, removing their power to hurt.

Ⓢ Three good things

Instead of letting these thoughts and emotions carry you away, for the next week focus on the bigger picture.

1 At the end of each day, before you go to sleep, write down three good things that happened to you in your notebook. These could be anything: someone smiled at you in the street, you found the necklace you thought you'd lost, you handed in a piece of work on time. Anything!

2 Reflect on why these things happened. Maybe the person smiled at you because you were smiling at them; perhaps you found your missing necklace because it was your lucky day; maybe you handed in your project on time because you worked incredibly hard.

Review: Properly paying attention to good things (by writing them down) is a simple way to lift your mood and stop NATs gaining a foothold. The reasons you attribute to the good things happening will make you see the world – and, by reflection, yourself – in a more positive light. People who appreciate what they have and who find reasons to be grateful tend to be happier, healthier, more optimistic and fulfilled. Studies show that gratitude can increase levels of wellbeing amongst those who cultivate it and people who undertook this strategy for just one week reported feeling happier up to six months later. There's no reason to stop at one week. If it's working for you build it into your daily routine.

Next steps ...

The next chapter looks at your mind's agendas and your own personal inner judge, who glories in telling you everything you're doing wrong. The internal rules and regulations you set for yourself shape your thoughts, NATs, mood and behaviour. Understanding how they all work together is integral to learning how to deal with them.

Thoughts to take away

✓ Thoughts aren't facts: they are just your mind's opinions and hypotheses

✓ Don't heedlessly believe the 'evidence' your mind presents you when you're under attack from NATs. Step back and take a fairer view

✓ Don't fall victim to the second arrow: your reactions can make things much worse (and, by the same token, much better if you react well!)

9b

The Right Frame of Mind

The mind produces lists of rules, expectations and standards it expects you to obey and uphold no matter what you're facing. This can spawn unhelpful judgements about yourself and others. Here you'll learn how to recognise which rules can and should be broken.

⑤ Mindfulness of an object

This strategy is adapted from *Teaching Clients to Use Mindfulness Skills*, Dunkley & Stanton.

For this strategy please go and find yourself a leaf. If you can't, then grab another small object (a stone, shell, pine cone, conker, twig, apple or coin) and replace the word 'leaf' below with whatever you've chosen.

Set your timer to 5 minutes and follow these observations. If your mind wanders, just bring it gently back to the strategy.

+ Hold the leaf in the palm of your hand, focusing on its weight. How heavy is it? Is it heavier in some places than others?
+ What does it feel like against the skin of your palm? Are there places where it touches and places where it doesn't?
+ Pick it up between your fingers and thumb. Notice the temperature of the leaf – does it feel warm or cool?
+ Notice the texture of the leaf – does it feel rough or smooth? Do the edges of the leaf feel the same as the middle? Is it hard or soft, firm or limp, damp or dry? What does the stalk feel like in comparison?
+ Allow your eye to follow the contour of the leaf, noticing its shape and size. View it from a variety of angles, seeing the shape change in your eyeline. How thin is it? How wide at its widest point?
+ Notice the colour on the upper side of the leaf, focusing on variations in shade and texture. Look at the detailing: any veins, ridges, patterns? Explore every part of the leaf: the edges, the middle, the stalk
+ Now, taking the leaf in your fingers, turn it over and notice how the underside differs in colour and texture. Notice how the light catches the leaf as you move it
+ Does the leaf have a particular smell? Is it more evident towards the stalk or in the body of the leaf and does it change if you run your nail over it?
+ Continue to use your senses to observe the leaf until the timer signals the end of the strategy

Review (in two parts):

1 First, how did you go about choosing your leaf (or whatever item you used)? Did you think, 'I want a good leaf' as you hunted for the perfect specimen? What were your definitions for a 'good leaf'? A 'good leaf' will vary from person to person. For example, some people might go for a dark-green healthy leaf, some yellow or red. Does it surprise you to realise you have a protocol for leaf-picking?

2 Did your mind wander during the analysis of the leaf? If so, where to? Did rules/conditions/expectations creep in, such as, 'I can't do that', 'I should do that'? Were you able to bring your mind back to the leaf? Did you notice any judgements creeping in: 'This is boring/pointless/useless'? Or any associations: 'This leaf reminds me of walking in the park yesterday'? Did you relive any memories in picture form? Did you experience any emotions – happiness, sadness, nostalgia or frustration?

Your mind's hidden agenda

We've discussed NATs, evidence-gathering and that devastating second arrow (see the previous chapter). The next stage in understanding what sets your mind-cogs in motion is being aware of its hidden agendas. As you've just experienced in the leaf strategy, your mind formulates a two-stage plan for whatever you're facing – a primary and secondary agenda:

+ **Your primary agenda:** What you're doing in the moment or plan to do
+ **Your secondary agenda:** The expectations, rules and conditions you have to follow when undertaking your primary agenda that dictate whether you succeed or fail

In the strategy, mindful study of a leaf was your primary agenda, however inevitably secondary 'hidden' agendas will have crept in: 'I have to get a good leaf. I can't think about anything else.' In focusing wholly on the leaf, you may have been more aware of when secondary agendas tried to interrupt ('I'm doing this wrong', 'My leaf is rubbish') so you could bat the thoughts away and bring your mind back to the task at hand.

Mindfulness is about allowing yourself to focus on your primary agenda, on what you're actually doing in the here and now, without allowing secondary agendas to cloud your focus. Your secondary agenda will try to butt in and create unnecessary parameters for success, but you can learn to recognise which are worth paying attention to and which should be dismissed out of hand. This will take practice because these rules, expectations and conditions have been permanent fixtures in your mind since you were a child. As discussed in Chapter 4 (see page 69), you'll have developed a belief system as you were growing up and it's these beliefs, on top of those gained through adult experience, that dictate how much you expect of yourself and what you consider important.

For example, imagine you're about to attend a parents' evening at your child's school – this is your primary agenda; your plan for the evening. However, instead of just going and hearing what the teachers have to say about your child's progress, your mind presents a secondary agenda which you don't question: 'I must wear an outfit that projects an aura of responsibility, yet sophistication. I can't make a fool of myself by cracking stupid jokes. I must avoid Joseph's parents because I can't remember their names'. Before you know it you've got a long list of rules to follow that will indelibly change how you experience the evening.

The leaf strategy makes you more aware of times you set boundaries for yourself so you can choose whether to adhere to them or not. So, the next time you're out and thoughts like, 'I can't say that,' or 'I'm wearing the wrong outfit' pop into your head, you won't simply agree and feel restricted, you'll be aware of what's happening and can then decide whether to pay attention to them or not. (See opposite for some more examples of situations that commonly present secondary agendas.)

A **Primary agenda:** Go out with colleagues for a post-work drink
  Secondary agenda: Don't moan about boss/complain about workload.
  Don't mention new job I'm going for. Laugh at Matthew's jokes
B **Primary agenda:** Attend family wedding
  Secondary agenda: Bring a great gift. Don't drink too much. Don't get
  stuck talking to Uncle Frank. Be nice to Horrible Susan
C **Primary agenda:** Go for job interview
  Secondary agenda: Be proud of my achievements, but not boastful
  Don't ask, 'How long do we get for lunch?' Cover up spot on nose

Mostly you accept secondary agendas without question because they've
come from your mind, so must be rooted in sense, right? Not necessarily.
They can be rooted in beliefs you've had for years that might not make
sense in the current context, but even if they are sensible, by following
them mindlessly your experience will always be restricted: 'How many
glasses of wine have I had? Was that a bad joke? There's Uncle Frank, quick
run away!' You might spend hours avoiding Uncle Frank when you could
have spoken to him for 20 minutes and got it over with. You've probably
noticed critical judgements colouring what you're doing during previous
strategies: 'I'm not doing it right', 'This is stupid', 'I need to try harder'.

Example: Beth's bad birthday

It was the day of Beth's 30th birthday party (primary agenda). Twenty-five
people were coming and she knew they'd bring extra guests, so there should
have been a good crowd. She was nervous, but excited. But two hours before
everyone was due to arrive, she got four cancellation texts within half an hour
from close friends who'd promised they'd come. 'No one's going to show up!'
she thought (NAT), quickly followed by, 'This is going to be rubbish (NAT).
I suppose if at least 15 people come it'll be OK. I'll just act as if I didn't ⋯⋮⋅

...⋮. expect any more than that and spend at least ten minutes with everyone. I should only drink gin and tonics and no wine as I tend to get silly on wine (secondary agendas)'.

Beth's primary agenda: Hosting her 30th birthday party
Beth's secondary agenda: Setting out rules that will determine whether the party is a success or not

Beth's mind map looks like this:

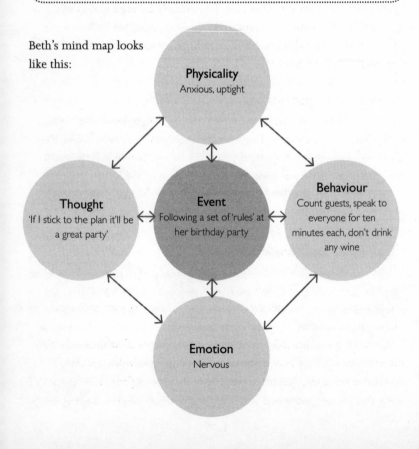

Physicality
Anxious, uptight

Thought
'If I stick to the plan it'll be a great party'

Event
Following a set of 'rules' at her birthday party

Behaviour
Count guests, speak to everyone for ten minutes each, don't drink any wine

Emotion
Nervous

Beth's secondary agenda is totally unnecessary. She's making life hard for herself and limiting her ability to enjoy her own party. She won't be fully 'present' at the party, because she'll be thinking, 'Are at least 15 people here? Have I spoken to everyone for at least ten minutes?' If you can't get silly on your 30th birthday, when can you? If she doesn't spend exactly ten minutes with everyone, who cares? They'll all know she's busy hosting. Beth set herself these rules as a way to judge whether the evening had been a success, as a kind of safety net, but she eliminated any chance of spontaneity and took the focus away from simply having a good time.

You can't stop your mind producing these agendas, but by becoming more aware of the rules you set yourself you'll be able to *choose* whether you want to follow them or not.

Your internal judge and jury

Secondary agendas are set by your own internal judgements of acceptability; your own measures of success and failure. By that same token, they also cause judgements because if you don't follow them correctly you'll have 'failed' in some way. Judgement: both cause and effect.

Judgements are tricky beasts. Some are fine – ones like, 'Driving with my lights off at night would be stupid' and 'Not answering the door to my mother-in-law would be rude'. Those kinds of judgements allow us to function without being arrested or starting a family war. However, negative judgements based on restrictive standards aren't useful and can be hugely damaging. They can cause low self-esteem and stamp the joy out of experiences. You can also start judging others by your own strict definitions of success.

Everyone has a tiny judge in their head who pipes up with pearls of so-called 'wisdom'. They have their own filing cabinet of rules, and shame on you if you fall short. This inner judge is the source of your NATs and is the voice that heckles you when you're feeling insecure: 'You're never going to manage, you're pathetic!' They love nothing better than goading you into believing you're doing things wrong or badly.

Unfortunately, your judge can be incredibly convincing because it only ever focuses on, and seems to confirm, long-held beliefs you hold about yourself. For example, if you've always felt overweight and unattractive your judge will dwell on those issues, picking out instances when you felt your worst and expounding on them until all sense of perspective is lost. Each thought chips away at your self-esteem and you end up creating unrealistic secondary agendas that set you up for a fall. For example, 'At dinner tonight, I will not eat any carbs' even though you're going to the local Italian where the chef always cooks your favourite pasta dish for you.

The very act of judging has a powerful influence on our ability to focus on the moment. If you're constantly assessing how well you're following 'the rules' you're never going to be present in the moment. You're taking away your freedom to choose what decisions to make and to live life fully. The judgements ('I'm doing this wrong'/'I can't do that'/'I have to follow my plan') hook you in and activate doing mode (see Chapter 7). You'll start thinking about what you need to change, how to fix things, who's to blame and how things should be different: ramping up your stress levels.

Example: Andy's argument

Andy and Carl had a stupid argument about money. They'd been friends for years and often had lighthearted 'debates' on topical subjects, but this one had got slightly out of hand. They both said things they regretted and parted on bad terms. A week later Carl sent Andy an email apologising and asking if they could forget it ever happened. Andy apologised too and agreed to draw a line under it. Except he couldn't. He kept going over and over the things Carl had said: 'I can't believe Carl said I wouldn't understand X, Y and Z! I would never have said something like that to him.'

Andy couldn't let the argument go because he was projecting his own standards of behaviour and expectations on Carl, who had never signed up to them. How many times have you thought: 'But I wouldn't do that' when someone upsets you? We all do it, but it's not actually fair. You're judging someone else according to your own personal rules, your own secondary agendas, which dictate what is and what isn't acceptable. Those are your rules, not theirs.

Realising and accepting this can lift a huge weight off your shoulders, as it stops you taking things so personally. Some people are forgetful and take things for granted. Some people are bolshy and opinionated. Some people aren't mindful and are totally wrapped up in themselves. It's not personal, they're just following their own rules, not yours.

Perfectionism

Perfection is a myth, it doesn't exist. Trying to measure up to an all-singing, all-dancing version of yourself will only make you anxious and sad as you'll never allow yourself to succeed. If you do reach your objective, you'll move the goalposts, constantly setting yourself unrealistic targets and then beating yourself up when you can't 'win'. You'll compare yourself to other people according to your own measures of success and failure, which will have an impact on those close to you. It'll also make you defensive, distant, irritable and confrontational as you're in thrall to your inner protocols, your secondary agendas and have completely lost sight of the here and now.

If you complete 99 per cent of a task well, but mess up 1 per cent you'll spend all your time dwelling on that 1 per cent, which is ridiculous. It's important to step back from a situation and take a view of the whole picture, not just what went wrong. A fair view would be to give 99 per cent of your attention to what went right and 1 per cent to what went wrong.

Here's another example: you come home after a busy day at work, open the fridge and find there's nothing in it except some mouldy cheese and a half-drunk bottle of vinegary wine. Your thoughts:

A 'Best go to the shops, then'

B 'I can't believe I forgot to buy dinner, what a moron! Now I'm going to have to go out in the rain. What an unbelievable waste of time'

C 'I can't believe my partner forgot to buy dinner, what an idiot! S/he never remembers anything! S/he's so selfish!'

In example A, your mind helped find a solution to the problem, but in B and C it took you down a very different, totally unhelpful, path. You have one negative thought ('I'm/he's such a moron'), which opens the door for a whole crowd of others to come crashing in.

We're not saying you should never make judgements. As previously mentioned, some judgements are essential to getting on in the world ('I shouldn't run across this motorway' / 'I shouldn't wear a suit to do the gardening'). They also form the basis of our moral code. Some things genuinely might be unacceptable to you and you don't agree with people who do them. That's perfectly reasonable. But loads of your internal judgements aren't useful in the slightest and you're probably not even aware you're using them as a yardstick to measure yourself and other people against.

Becoming more aware of your judgements will give you the ability to decide whether they're actually helpful or not. Are they making you feel better or worse? By noticing the judgements you can step back from them and get some perspective, giving you a choice in what comes next.

⑤ Counting your judgements

For one day try to notice each and every time you say or think something judgemental about yourself or others. Then ask yourself these questions:

+ What was my exact thought? Keep it simple and don't get too deeply into it. For example: 'This is rubbish', 'He's such a fool'
+ Next, try to work out the tone of voice you're saying it in – yes, even in your head. Are you sneering, shouting, whispering? Tone can be used as an early-warning sign ('I'm about to be judgemental…')
+ What is your body language saying? These thoughts or spoken words will affect your body. For example, you might cross your arms or roll your eyes. (You can work backwards if needs be. If you noticed negative body language at any point, go back to the thought that prompted it.)
+ Make an on-going tally in your notebook every time you make a judgement
+ As you notice them, ask yourself 'Is this helpful'? If not, then let it go
+ As you notice yourself being judgemental make sure you don't judge yourself for it!

Review: Were you surprised by how many judgements you made and what they were? Did you notice a pattern to your judgements, for example, were many about appearance or social graces or work rate?

This exercise is designed to make you more aware of judgements as they flit in and out of your head, since often we're not even aware of them. By identifying them you'll be able to choose whether to give them any headspace or not.

Remember: Thoughts aren't facts

A key part to feeling better is changing your relationship with your thoughts – your NATs and judgements (or judgemental NATs) aren't facts. They are fleeting evaluations that you can choose to engage with or not. Thoughts come and go. They do not define you. You are not your thoughts!

Getting the full story on judgements

Often our evaluating thoughts (including judgements and NATs) are short, concise and to the point, for example: 'I'm a fraud'. What a terrible all-encompassing statement to make about yourself. If a friend said this about themselves would you just accept it as a statement of fact? No, you'd ask for more details. By investigating and fleshing out your judgements and the shorthand your mind uses you'll become more mindful. By getting more information you'll be more focused on the present and what's going on in your head. To do this you need to start giving things mindful descriptions, so you get to the truth of the matter and stick to the facts.

Here is a table listing some examples that illustrate how the mind's shorthand rarely gives us a true picture of what's actually happened.

Thought	Mindful description
'I'm a bad parent'	'I forgot a school meeting'
'I'm such an embarrassment'	'I tripped up in front of strangers'
'I'm no good at anything'	'I failed my driving test'
'My boss thinks I'm stupid'	'My boss didn't reply to my last email'
'My partner is fed up with me'	'My partner snapped at me when s/he was running late'
'Everything's awful'	'I've got so much work on that I can't meet my friends tonight'

Ⓢ Describing things mindfully

Draw out your own table and for one day write down any NATs and/or judgements you have about yourself. Don't use any emotive language, just stick to the facts, i.e. don't write, 'My partner snapped at me for no reason', instead write 'My partner snapped at me'. Then, fill in the 'mindful descriptions column with more information. Ask yourself, 'What *actually* happened?'

Taking your new mindful descriptions into account, take a step back from the original thought and don't allow that second arrow (see pages 142–3) to hurt you more.

Review: This strategy should show you the gap between fleeting thoughts and reality. Judgements and secondary agendas summarise complicated events and emotions into shorthand which, more often than not, isn't helpful and which triggers self-recrimination cycles. Being aware of this will help you to step back rather than automatically be drawn in.

Thoughts to take away

✓ Your mind has protocols for everything. Becoming more aware of these secondary agendas will allow you to choose whether you want to follow them or not

✓ Noticing what your inner judge is saying will enable you to step back from unrealistic expectations, self-criticism and criticism of others so you can get a fairer perspective

✓ Getting into the habit of describing things mindfully will show you how often your thoughts are exaggerating internal fears without representing reality. Get the facts!

10

It Crossed my Mind

Your thoughts can attach themselves to you like leeches, sucking up all your confidence and self-esteem. In this chapter you'll learn to identify the types of thoughts that trigger upsetting moods and learn how to extinguish their emotional power.

Clinging to your thoughts

Thoughts don't just colour your mood, they are also coloured by your mood, for example, the thought: 'I can't do this' will make you feel anxious, just as if you're already feeling anxious you're more likely to think, 'I can't do this'. It's a two-way street.

When you're experiencing a strong emotion, you can become attached to your thoughts – they validate how you feel, so you cling to them. The phrase 'lost in your thoughts' is apt. You become so caught up in this soup of feelings, thoughts, judgements, justifications and hidden agendas that before you know it you've staggered onto the train to Nowhere Good and are being taken for a ride.

Ⓢ The thoughts credit reel

+ Think of a difficult situation you've experienced recently
+ Imagine that those thoughts are being projected on to a big cinema screen, rolling through like the credits at the end of a film
+ Picture yourself sitting back in your seat, away from the screen, watching the credits roll. Don't challenge or change the thoughts, just notice them as they scroll past

Review: What happened to the thoughts? Did they appear and then disappear? Most people find that their thoughts come…and then go. They don't have to loiter around. We tend to cling on to negative thoughts much more than we do positive ones. When you're feeling great, you don't stop to ponder, 'I wonder why I'm feeling this good?' you just enjoy the feeling. However, when you feel bad you want to know why, so you start analysing your mood and thoughts (activating doing mode). Stop it! You don't have to wade into bad thoughts; you can just acknowledge them and then let them go.

Ⓢ Emotion overload

The next time you feel a strong emotion, tune into it and write down all the thoughts you're having in your notebook.

For example, Clare is planning to hand in her notice at work tomorrow before setting off on a six-month trip around the world. Her stomach is in knots and her thoughts are a jumble of 'what ifs' and NATs. She starts the strategy and writes down:

+ What if I never get such a good job again?
+ What if I'm not cut out for travelling and wish I'd never gone?
+ I'll inevitably lose my passport again like I did in Thailand five years ago
+ My parents won't be able to cope without me

Review: Writing down your thoughts forces you to slow down and pay attention to them. It's all too easy to let them pile up on top of each other until they're a throbbing pile of dread. This strategy forces you to see them (actually physically see them because you've written them down) as individual culprits, giving you some much needed distance. The pause between having the thought and writing it down will give you a calmer perspective because you feel more in control: 'I'm doing something about how I feel'. You can then go through your thoughts one by one to work out whether they have any merit and whether you want to spend any time on them.

Labelling your thoughts

By now you should be becoming a bit of an expert on your own mind. You're familiar with the stories your mind tells you as well as NATs, judgements and hidden agendas. You can tune in to your mood and untangle the thoughts that are both causing it and prolonging it. You also know that a thought isn't automatically true just because you thought it, even if you don't always put this knowledge into practice.

Some thoughts can really dig their claws in, getting under your skin and making you do things that are out of character or that make things worse. A really simple and useful tactic for putting distance between yourself and your thoughts is to label them.

The train analogy we used at the start of the chapter is an effective one. Imagine that each thought you have is a train clattering through a station. Before you started this process you would have leapt on board every one, and, before you knew it, you'd be stuck at Paranoia Central without a return ticket.

By labelling your thoughts you're ensuring that each train has a clearly signposted destination, giving you a choice about whether to board or not. This means that the next time a train whooshes in signposted Hair-Pulling Anxiety you won't automatically jump on or, worse, throw yourself in front of it. Instead, you'll be able to choose. Choice is the Holy Grail as far as mindfulness is concerned. You're giving yourself the options to make informed choices about whether you want to engage with your thoughts. If they're unhelpful, damaging or untrue, you can just watch that train go past without getting on. The train/thought will then disappear.

⑤ Voice your thoughts (part 1)

This strategy is adapted from *Teaching Clients to Use Mindfulness Skills*, Dunkley & Stanton.

Set your timer for two minutes. Sit in the recommended meditative pose (see page 47) then get into your head. Pay attention to any thought that passes through your mind and say it out loud starting with: 'I am noticing the thought…'. Thoughts can come as words or images – say them all. There's no right or wrong, no bad thoughts or good thoughts, no judgement. For example, 'I am noticing the thought that this seems a strange thing to do. I am noticing the thought that saying, "I am noticing the thought" seems odd. I am noticing the thought that I can't think of

anything. I am noticing the thought that my mind seems totally blank.
I am noticing the thought that my mind just flicked to a film I watched
recently. I am noticing the thought that I'm wondering how long I've been
doing this for. I am noticing the thought that I need to call my mum. I am
noticing the thought that I'm quite hungry.'

⑤ Voice your thoughts (part 2)

Now add a label to each thought, for example: 'I am noticing a
judgemental thought: This seems stupid'; 'I am noticing a planning
thought: I need to get some chicken for dinner'; 'I am noticing a worrying
thought: What if work is rubbish tomorrow?'; 'I am noticing a dwelling
thought: Why did I tell that awful story at dinner last night?'

Review: How did you find this – easier or harder than expected?

Labelling your thoughts slows them down – a key part of mindfulness.
Slowing down means instead of always acting on gut instincts you can
consciously decide how you want to engage with a situation. Taking things
slowly also limits how much you'll be driven by your emotions. It's the
same theory behind the emotion overload strategy (see page 163) in
which you wrote your thoughts down. By labelling them you're distancing
yourself from them. Your judgement thoughts, worry thoughts and
dwelling thoughts will lose their emotional power if you allow yourself
some perspective.

If you can see your thoughts as passing events that come and go they
can't hurt you, bully you, cajole you or set secondary agendas without
your permission. Which is pretty damn exciting as far as we're concerned.

A broken record

Once you become more practised at labelling your thoughts you might
start to notice that some come up again and again, especially when you're

in a bad mood, stressed, anxious or low. You may also have noticed them knocking on the door of your mind during a meditation. Once you realise these are the same thoughts that pop up regularly, you won't need to rise to the bait any more.

A simple way of getting used to labelling recurring thoughts is to imagine them as a music playlist. Your habitual negative thought patterns are like a broken record or bad music selection going round and round on repeat, telling you the same old story. For example, you're feeling hurt, so turn on the 'This always happens to me' playlist, featuring tracks such as: 'They always treat me badly' or 'Why can't things be different?' By categorising your thoughts as certain playlists you'll get better at identifying them and knowing when to turn them off. Some example playlists:

+ The 'Everyone has it easier than me' playlist
+ The 'No one recognises how hard I work' playlist
+ The 'I can't stand my colleague' playlist
+ The 'This is all my fault' playlist
+ The 'I always say the wrong thing' playlist

Within these playlists are any number of individual 'songs' (thoughts). For example, on the 'I always say the wrong thing' playlist you might have:

+ 'I always put my foot in it with Michelle'
+ 'Why can I never think of a witty retort until two hours later?'
+ 'I can't believe I told that dreadful story to my boss'
+ 'I'm better off just staying at home so I don't embarrass myself'
+ 'I can't believe I missed my chance to ask for a pay rise'

S Your top ten playlists

A Write down your top ten playlists. The negative thinking patterns that come up time and time again. If you're struggling, think back to a recent time when you felt stressed, angry or unhappy and work from there.

Here are some more examples that might ring a bell:

1 'I'm a fraud'
2 'Is this all there is to life?'
3 'I don't earn enough money'
4 'I'm really unappreciated'
5 'My life isn't going anywhere'
6 'I'll never meet the love of my life'
7 'I'm not attractive enough'
8 'I hate my boss'
9 'I'm better than this'
10 'Something has to change'

B Next, write down some of the individual thoughts that make up the songs on the playlists. For example, under 'I'm a fraud' perhaps you often think: 'I'm going to be found out'; 'I don't know what I'm doing'; 'I'm not qualified for this'.

C Finally, read back through each playlist, one track at a time, and try to identify the feelings that accompanied each thought. Fill in the table below, asking yourself how the playlists make you feel emotionally and physically and what you think you can do to help. (We have used a table to save space, but you could draw out individual mind maps if you'd find that easier. However, remember to change the 'Behaviour' section to 'What can I do to help'?)

Thought	Emotions	Physicality	What can I do to help?
'I'm a fraud'	Nervous, anxious	Fidgety, shaky, twitchy, heart racing	Meditate to give myself more focus
'Something has to change'	Low, despondent, trapped	Heavy, exhausted, sluggish	Take time for myself, ask for help, slow down

Review: By categorising your thoughts, you're removing their power to hurt you. If you continue to let these broken records play over and over again, you'll feel bad. That's a fact. It's like watching a movie you've seen 15 times. You know what happens next, but you carry on watching regardless. You'll start blaming yourself or others for not living up to the rules in your head – rules that restrict you. You'll also strike yourself with a second arrow (see pages 142–3) if something bad happens. (Remember, second arrows are self-inflicted: you don't have to fire them; you don't have to make a tough situation tougher.)

If you don't like the playlist analogy, don't worry. Think of another or just stick to simple labels: 'dwelling thoughts/judgement thoughts/ self-blame thoughts'. Whatever works for you. The point is that you're recognising them and in doing so, you're taking control.

Example: Steph's self-blame playlist

When tidying up, Steph noticed a letter peeping out from under a pile of mail. Her heart dropped. She knew what it was – a final electricity bill reminder. She ripped it open and gasped. The payment had been due last week and if she didn't pay she would be cut off…in two days! She hadn't meant to skip paying, she was just disorganised. 'I can't believe I've done this!' she raged to herself. 'I'm such an IDIOT. I can't even pay my bills on time – I'm pathetic!'

She started practising the strategies from Chapters 9a and 9b, identifying her thoughts and then labelling them. The next time she forgot a bill, the same routine started again. 'Steph, you're so unbelievably stupid,' she shouted at herself before taking a deep breath. She thought, 'This is my self-blame playlist. I know what happens next so I'm going to stop.' Doing this gave her perspective: the bottom line was that the bill needed paying. Ranting and raving wasn't going to pay it. She phoned the company, calmly, and paid.

Stop trying so hard

We want you to stop trying to fight your thoughts. Starting a war won't make you feel calmer or more in control. The next strategy will let you disengage from thoughts, to let the thought train appear... then disappear, without any rioting on board. This will cause a positive, domino effect on your mood, behaviour and body. It's a step on from the sounds meditation in Chapter 7 (see page 113), building thoughts into the practice.

Ⓢ Sounds and thoughts

This strategy is pretty long (approximately 15–20 minutes) so we'd recommend recording it so you can listen as you go along.

Settling with breath and body

1 Sit in the recommended meditation position (see page 47) with your shoulders relaxed, head and neck balanced and chin tucked in slightly.
2 Bring your attention to the movements of the breath in the body for a few minutes, until you feel settled, then expand your attention to take in the body as a whole, as if the whole body were breathing, helping you to be aware of all the sensations you're experiencing.
3 Spend a few minutes practising mindfulness of the breath and body in this way, remembering that you can always use them as an anchor if your mind becomes too distracted or overwhelmed.

Sounds

4 When you're ready, allow the focus of your attention to shift from sensations in the body to the sounds around you.
5 There is no need to go searching for sounds or listening out for anything in particular. Instead, as best you can, simply remain receptive to sounds from all directions as they arise – near, far, in front, behind, to the side, above or below you. Open up to the 'soundscape' around you.

Perhaps notice how the obvious sounds can easily crowd out the more subtle ones. Are there spaces between sounds, any moments of quiet?

6 Try to be aware of the sounds as raw sensations. Notice the tendency we have to categorise them (for example: car, train, voice, radio), and see if it's possible to notice this habit and then refocus on what you're hearing.

7 If you start thinking about the sounds ('There's a fire engine – what's on fire?'), try to focus on sensory qualities (patterns of pitch, timbre, loudness, duration), rather than meanings, implications or associations.

8 Whenever you notice that your awareness is no longer focused on what you're hearing, gently acknowledge where your mind has moved to and then retune it to sounds as they arise and fade, moment to moment.

9 Focus on sounds for 4 or 5 minutes before moving on.

Thoughts

10 Shift your focus of attention so your thoughts are centre-stage, seeing them, as best you can, as events in the mind.

11 Notice when your thoughts appear, as they linger in the space of the mind (like clouds moving across the sky). Eventually, see if you can detect the moment they dissolve.

12 There is no need to try to make thoughts come or go. In the same way that you related to the arising and passing away of sounds, just let thoughts appear and pass on their own.

13 Just as clouds moving across the sky are sometimes dark and stormy, sometimes light and fluffy, so thoughts take different forms.

14 Alternatively, pay attention to the thoughts as credits at the end of a film as you did in the previous strategy. As the thoughts scroll past, pay attention to them when they're 'on screen', and then stop as they disappear. Notice when you get drawn in and find yourself up there on screen too. Congratulate yourself for noticing you're trying to get involved in the film, then return to your seat and wait patiently for the

next sequence of thoughts to arise.

15 If thoughts bring intense emotions, pleasant or unpleasant, try to note their 'emotional charge' ('what am I feeling?) and then let both the thought and feeling go.

16 If you feel your mind has become unfocused and scattered, or you keep getting drawn into stories, focus on your breath and sense of the whole body, anchoring and stabilising awareness back to the present.

Review: How did you find the strategy? Hopefully, through your previous practice of the sound meditation in Chapter 7 (see page 113), you will have found it easier to tune into the sounds you're hearing. However, the thoughts part may have been tricky – it's easy to get sucked into tales, associations and evaluations. The aim of this meditation is to start seeing the similarities between sound and thought: both appear from nowhere, both trigger emotions, associations and evaluations and both disappear as fast as they appear. You can start separating your reactions – here's a sound, a thought, a feeling – while keeping a respectable distance from them.

Thoughts to take away

✓ Your emotions and thoughts are intrinsically connected. Use your mood as a guide to rooting out distressing thoughts

✓ Labelling your thoughts is a simple way of reducing their power, stopping them from sneaking in and getting under your skin

✓ Viewing thoughts as similar to sounds will give you distance: they are both transient events that come and go

A final message

Congratulations! You've completed this introduction to mindfulness, which dipped and delved into some pretty intense places. We hope through practising the strategies you've noticed a difference in your life – how you feel emotionally and physically day-to-day. Hopefully your outlook is more positive and you feel more present. In its simplest form mindfulness snaps you out of autopilot, making experiences more meaningful, so that everything becomes brighter, more vivid and real. This is truly something to be celebrated.

To measure how far you've come, try answering these questions:

1 **After reading the book – how do you feel?**

    A The same – no change

    B A smidgen better – starting to think this all through

    C Better – seeing gradual improvements

    D Amazing – transformed

If you answered A did you really invest all your energy in the strategies? Are you willing to try them again? Becoming mindful takes work and old habits are hard to break. Open your mind to new things and then practise, practise, practise! If the theory makes sense then the practical parts will follow with time. If you answered B–D then we're very chuffed for you. Keep up the good work!

2a **Which strategies did you find easier to grasp and which harder?** Stay with the easier ones for a while and build confidence with these and then retry the harder ones. The strategies build through the book and the earlier meditations give you the foundations for the harder ones.

2b **Which strategies did you find worked best for which situations and which mood?** Did you find the body scan helped you switch to being mode? Did the rejecting rejection strategy in Chapter 8 help you to deal with sadness? Be sure to utilise certain strategies for specific situations. Thinking about how they helped will encourage you to use them in day-to-day life.

3 **Which of the Thoughts to Take Away listed at the bottom of each chapter particularly struck a chord?** Write them down so that every time you need a pick-me-up, or a kick up the backside, you can flick through and motivate yourself.

4 **Are you going to be more aware of times when you're ruminating on the past (dwelling on regrets), rather than reflecting (using what you've learned to move on)?**

5 **Are you going to pay attention to your body, using physical cues to tune into your emotional state and vice versa?**

6 **Are you going to be aware of your mind's secondary agendas to choose whether you want to follow the rules it's set you or not?** Will you be more sceptical of your inner judge when it's spouting judgements? Will you also remember that others haven't signed up to your internal rule book, so you might have to cut them some slack?

7 **Are you going to remember the danger of the second arrow when you feel upset, stressed, low or anxious?**

8 **Will you be more aware of NATs when they start masquerading as facts in your head?** (Always remember: thoughts aren't facts!)

9 **How will you build mindfulness into your life? Can you put aside a regular time for formal practice?** By doing this you're more likely to incorporate informal mindfulness into your day-to-day experience.

10 **When are you going to start thinking differently?**

    A I already have   C Tomorrow

    B Today   D Never

These questions aren't intended to stress you out – there are no right or wrong answers. You can use them to assess how you feel now, whether there are areas of mindfulness you want to concentrate on and whether it has, in fact, made a difference to your life. It's also a way of seeking out doubts or scepticism that might be holding you back. You have the tools to become more mindful; how and whether you use them is up to you. It's hard, but rewarding. And it works.

If there are bits of the book you haven't tackled yet, don't worry, just go back and give them a go. Refer back to the list of reasons you gave for starting this journey in Chapter 1 to encourage yourself to keep at it.

Unfortunately, you can't get rid of stress, anxiety and low mood completely, they're a part of life – but that doesn't mean they should rule your life. This is why it's important to practise mindfulness all the time, when you're feeling good as well as bad. If you try to be mindful all the time, the techniques will become second nature, so you'll employ them automatically when things get tough. Mindfulness will make good things better and bad things more bearable.

This is all about making changes that last. Of course there'll be times when you slip up, when you find it hard and really just want to rant, moan, worry and dwell on regrets. That's natural. Don't beat yourself up for not being mindful. Instead congratulate yourself on noticing that's what happened. Having the ability to recognise what your mind is doing and what it's already done is mindfulness at its very essence. You can then step back, get some perspective and choose how to proceed.

Mindfulness is about awareness. Awareness of yourself both mentally and physically, awareness of your choices, awareness of other people and awareness of the world. Life doesn't have to pass you by, it can be lived moment by moment in full technicolour rather than dull grey. You can choose to make life worthwhile, memorable and meaningful. It's enormously liberating and powerful to have that ability and that choice.

Good luck with everything and please let us know how you get on at www.jessamyandjo.com.

Further reading

Thích Nhât Hạnh, *The Miracle of Mindfulness: The Classic Guide to Meditation by the World's Most Revered Master* (Ebury Publishing, 2008)

Mark Williams, *Mindfulness: A Practical Guide to Finding Peace in a Frantic World* (Piatkus, 2011)

Mark Williams, John Teasdale, Zindel Segal and Jon Kabat-Zinn, *The Mindful Way Through Depression: Freeing Yourself from Chronic Unhappiness* (Guilford Press, 2007)

John Teasdale, Mark Williams and Zindel Segal, *The Mindful Way Workbook: An 8-week Program to Free Yourself from Depression and Emotional Distress* (Guilford Press, 2013)

Christine Dunkley and Maggie Stanton, *Teaching Clients to Use Mindfulness Skills: A Practical Guide* (Routledge, 2013)

Useful websites

MIND, The National Association for Mental Health: www.mind.org.uk
Time to Change: www.time-to-change.org.uk
Frantic World: www.franticworld.com
Be Mindful: www.bemindful.co.uk
Mood Gym: www.moodgym.anu.edu.au
Living Life to the Full: www.llttf.com
The Centre for Clinical Interventions: www.cci.health.wa.gov.au
The Mental Health Foundation: www.mentalhealth.org.uk
American Mental Health Foundation: www.americanmentalhealthfoundation.org
The Beck Institute: www.beckinstitute.org
Cruse Bereavement Care: www.cruse.org.uk
Relate: www.relate.org.uk/home/index.html
Frank, friendly confidential drugs advice: www.talktofrank.com
Alcohol Concern: www.alcoholconcern.org.uk
The British Psychological Society: www.bps.org.uk
The British Association for Behavioural & Cognitive Psychotherapy:
    www.babcp.com
Samaritans: www.samaritans.org

Acknowledgements

We have so much gratitude for everyone who believed in these books and helped to make them happen. A huge thanks to our wonderful families, especially Ben, Jack, Max and Edie. To Marc Balint for his mindfulness expertise and support, Christine Dunkley and Maggie Stanton for their brilliant workshop and mindfulness exercises and Mark Lau at the Vancouver CBT Centre for his teachings and advice. We'd also like to thank Kerry Enzor and Richard Green at Quercus for their unfaltering enthusiasm, our agent Jane Graham Maw for her encouragement, and Jo Godfrey Wood and Peggy Sadler at Bookworx for their unsurpassed editing and design skills.

References

P.72: Exercise adapted from 'Lengthening the Breath' from Thích Nhât Nạnh, *The Miracle of Mindfulness* (Ebury Publishing, 2008) (permission to use exercise, pages 18–19)

P.77: Raisin exercise adapted from Mark Williams, John Teasdale, Zindel Segal and Jon Kabat-Zinn, *The Mindful Way Through Depression: Freeing Yourself from Chronic Unhappiness* (Guilford Press, 2007) (permission to use 'The Raisin Exercise', Box, pages 55–6)

P.111: Feet think/feel exercise adapted from *The Mindful Way Through Depression*, ibid. (permission to use 'Doing mode vs. Being mode', page 100)

P.115: Doing vs Being mode table adapted from John Teasdale, Mark Williams and Zindel Segal, *The Mindful Way Workbook: An 8-Week Program to Free Yourself from Depression and Emotional Distress* (Guilford Press, 2013) (permission to use 'Doing vs being mode', pages 22–5)

P.116: 3-minute breathing space adapted from Zindel Segal, Mark Williams and John Teasdale, *Mindfulness-Based Cognitive Therapy for Depression*, Second Edition (Guilford Press, 2012) (permission to use '3 minute breathing space, Session 3 – Handout 2', page 208)

P.127: Table adapted from *The Mindful Way Through Depression*, ibid. (permission to use 'Inviting a difficulty in and working with it through the body', Box, pages 151–2)

P.169: Exercise adapted from *The Mindful Way Through Depression*, ibid. (permission to use 'Mindfulness of hearing and thinking', Box, pages 166–8)